Daily *warm-ups*

WORLD RELIGIONS

WESTERN EDUCATIONAL ACTIVITIES LTD.
12006 - 111 Ave. Edmonton, Alberta T5G 0E8
Ph: (780) 413-7055   Fax: (780) 413-7056
GST : R105636187

WALCH PUBLISHING

1   2   3   4   5   6   7   8   9   10

ISBN 0-8251-5083-3

Copyright © 2004

Walch Publishing

P. O. Box 658 • Portland, Maine 04104-0658

walch.com

Printed in the United States of America

Table of Contents

Introduction   *iv*

The *Daily Warm-Ups* series is a wonderful way to turn extra classroom minutes into valuable learning time. The 180 quick activities—one for each day of the school year—address issues of character. These daily activities may be used at the very beginning of class to get students into learning mode, near the end of class to make good educational use of that transitional time, in the middle of class to shift gears between lessons—or whenever else you have minutes that now go unused. In addition to presenting students with the basic themes of character education, they are a natural path to other classroom activities involving critical thinking.

Daily Warm-Ups are easy-to-use reproducibles—simply photocopy the day's activity and distribute it. Or make a transparency of the activity and project it on the board. You may want to use the activities to reinforce student awareness of character issues and to promote critical-thinking skills that are built and acquired over time.

However you choose to use them, *Daily Warm-Ups* are a convenient and useful supplement to your regular lesson plans. Make every minute of your class time count!

What Year Is It?

Did you know that our concept of time is affected by religion? The calendar we use in the United States is called the Gregorian calendar. It is named for Pope Gregory XIII. This calendar was developed for use by the Christian Church. It marks years as beginning with the birth of Christ. The abbreviation B.C. means "before Christ." The abbreviation A.D. means *anno Domini,* or "in the year of the Lord." Today, we often use the term *Common Era* (C.E.) instead of A.D. and *before the Common Era* (B.C.E.) for B.C.

In contrast, the Islamic calendar used in some Islamic countries marks years as beginning with the Hegira, the year that Muhammad emigrated from Mecca to Medina. The abbreviation A.H. means *anno Hegirae,* or "in the year of the Hegira." The year A.H. 1 is the same as A.D. 622.

Other countries use their own official calendars with different months and years.

Do you think countries should use a calendar rooted in religion? Or should all countries follow a secular (nonreligious) calendar? Write two or three sentences for your answer.

Daily Warm-Ups: World Religions

1

Religions Around the World

These are the ten world religions with the greatest number of followers. Number them from 1 to 10 according to the number of followers each has, with 1 having the most and 10 the least. How many of these religions are you familiar with?

Baha'i: _____

Buddhism: _____

Chinese traditional religion (including Taoism): _____

Christianity: _____

Hinduism: _____

Islam: _____

Jainism: _____

Judaism: _____

Sikhism: _____

Spiritualism: _____

2

Spirituality in Your Life

Does your daily life have elements of a spiritual, philosophical, or religious path? If so, how do these elements affect the way you act and the decisions you make? If not, why do you think that is? Write two or three sentences for your answer.

General

Beliefs and Values

Simply put, religion tells us how we can live and what is important. Religion offers us a way to understand life.

List some of the values or goals of your religion. If you do not belong to a religious tradition, list some personal values. What do you believe in? What beliefs or values guide the choices you make?

4

Benefits of Religion

Religion can be defined as a belief in a superhuman power. Religions usually feature a code of values, which often includes a certain set of moral and ethical obligations. People who are religious follow a path of worship based on these obligations with the hope of attaining profound benefits from their practice.

Describe something you do that is deeply gratifying but not religious. Does this thing change your life in the way religion can? What benefits do you derive from it?

Daily Warm-Ups: World Religions

5

© 2004 Walch Publishing

Hinduism

Origins of Hinduism

Hinduism developed over a long period of time; although the religion is about 3,000 years old, some elements are much older. Hinduism is not based on the teachings or words of any one person. Although there have been many teachers within Hinduism, it has no single fundamental teacher and no prophets. Hinduism does not have one holy book that lays out the tenets of the religion. It combines ideas from different cultures and periods.

In what ways does this make Hinduism different from other major world religions, such as Christianity, Islam, Judaism, and Taoism? Write one or two sentences for your answer.

6

Hinduism

Facts About Hinduism

Here are some facts about Hinduism. Use them to write an informational paragraph about this ancient religion. Use the space below.

- Has about 800 million followers worldwide

- Has no founder or prophets

- Not a single, unified religion

- About 80% of the population of India considers themselves Hindus

- Over 3,000 years old

- Includes the concept of a cycle of birth, death, and rebirth

- Has many deities, including Krishna, Shiva, and Rama

7

Hinduism

The Spread of Hinduism

About 3,000 years ago, Hinduism began near the Indus River of northwestern India. It spread throughout India and across East Asia. Although many of the countries in this region later adopted Buddhism or Islam as their primary religion, Hindu influence is still seen in the culture and literature of much of Southeast Asia. Today Nepal is the only official Hindu state in the world. (Although many Indians are Hindu, India has no official state religion.)

Find Nepal on a map. Why do you think this country has stayed primarily Hindu, while other countries converted to other religions?

8

Hinduism

Hinduism or Sanatana Dharma?

Hinduism is the Western name for traditional Indian religion. The Indian name is Sanatana Dharma, or "Universal Religion." The word *Hindu* is probably a Persian mispronunciation of "Sindhu," another name for the Indus River. This name was first used for traditional Indian religion in the early 1800s. Since then, it has become the accepted English term.

Think about other instances where ideas from one culture are given a different name by another culture. How would you react if an idea that is important to you were referred to by a different name? Do you think it is appropriate to use our own words for ideas from other cultures, or should we use the original culture's terms? Write two or three sentences to explain your answer.

9

Hinduism

Daily Warm-Ups: World Religions

Terms in Hinduism

All religions have terms with special meanings. Here are some terms used in Hinduism. Some of these terms have been adopted into English. However, some have different meanings in English. Draw a line from each term to the best definition of its meaning within Hinduism.

1. atman

2. dharma

3. guru

4. karma

5. samsara

6. yoga

a. the cosmic law of cause and effect, where good deeds lead to positive effects

b. the soul; the essence of a person

c. a technique for attaining spiritual realization

d. a spiritual teacher or guide

e. the moral and ethical aims of life

f. the endless cycle of death and rebirth

10

© 2004 Walch Publishing

Hinduism

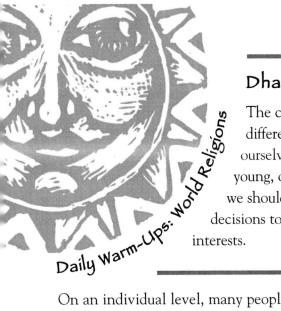

Dharma

The concept of *dharma* is important in Hinduism. Dharma has several different meanings. Following our dharma involves conducting ourselves righteously and according to our role in life. When we are young, our role in life is to be a good son or daughter. As we grow older, we should be good students, good friends, good citizens. When we have decisions to make, we should do what is right, even if it goes against our best interests.

On an individual level, many people—consciously or unconsciously—do act in this way. But on a global level, people often put their own interests first. Think of a situation (either from history or from current events) where a person or a country acted based on self-interest rather than on what is right. Describe the situation. Then say what the person or the country should have done. How would that have affected history or current events?

11

Hinduism

Transmigration of Souls

In the Hindu view of life, the soul is not permanently attached to one body. A soul first enters the world in the body of a simple life form—not a human. When that first body dies, the soul moves on to a more complex life form and is reborn there. This has been compared to the way people outgrow clothes and need new ones. The process of rebirth is called *samsara*. The Bhagavad Gita, part of a Hindu epic, says

Worn-out garments are shed by the body; worn-out bodies are shed by the dweller.

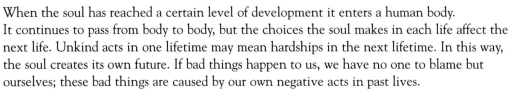

When the soul has reached a certain level of development it enters a human body. It continues to pass from body to body, but the choices the soul makes in each life affect the next life. Unkind acts in one lifetime may mean hardships in the next lifetime. In this way, the soul creates its own future. If bad things happen to us, we have no one to blame but ourselves; these bad things are caused by our own negative acts in past lives.

12

If people are responsible for their own futures, what would be the best way to act in this lifetime? Write two or three sentences for your answer.

The Soul

Shankaracharya was a Hindu teacher who founded four great monasteries in India. He once explained that humans are like jars filled with air. Our souls are the air. This air is the same as the air outside the jar. When the jar breaks at death, the inside air joins the outside air.

Think about this description for a minute or two. Then write three or four sentences giving your reaction to it.

13

Hinduism

The Law of Karma

In the Hindu view of the world, souls go through an endless process of death and rebirth. Our actions in this life affect the next life. This is called the law of *karma*.

In a way, we can look at karma as cause and effect. Every individual action has an effect, either good, neutral, or bad. If we live a life of good deeds, good things will eventually happen to us—if not in this life, then in the next one. If we are selfish and narrow-minded, then bad things will happen to us.

In this way of thinking, there are no such things as accidents or luck—either good luck or bad luck. Everything that happens is the result of some action we took either in this life or one in the past.

14

Think about something unexpected that happened to you recently, either good or bad. Describe the incident. Did you think it was an accident or "just luck"? Would your attitude toward the event change if you thought your own past actions had caused it? Explain.

Karma: Fatalism, or Complete Control?

According to the Hindu law of karma, a person's future is determined by his or her past actions. Some people interpret this as meaning that humans are controlled by fate. We don't really have control of what happens to us in this life, as the outcome has already been set.

Other people interpret the law of karma as meaning that humans have complete control. If we focus on what we do in the present, we can ensure good things in our future. We also have control of the way we react to things in the present. A negative event may have been caused by a negative act that we committed in the past. If we react to it in a negative way—with anger, for example, or with a selfish focus—this reaction may cause yet another negative event in the future. But if we respond in a positive way, not getting angry but accepting the event as part of life, the future effect may be positive.

Can you identify with either of these ideas of life—controlled by fate or controlled by our own actions? Choose one of these ideas. Then write two or three sentences about how this idea of life might affect the way you act.

15

Daily Warm-Ups: World Religions

Hinduism

Brahman, the Universal Spirit

We often think of Hinduism as having many gods. However, Hindu beliefs also include the concept of *Brahman*, the universal spirit. Brahman permeates everything, and everything is part of Brahman. Our souls are part of Brahman and seek to be reunited with him. Brahman is infinite and eternal—and impossible to describe.

Since people think in concrete terms, most find it hard to imagine divinity on this scale, with no form or face. For this reason, some Hindus believe that Brahman is manifested in many different forms, some of which are gods. Since Brahman is in everything, including us, then Brahman is also in the different gods of Hinduism. In the Bhagavad Gita, part of a great Hindu epic, the god Krishna says, "Whatever god a man worships, it is I who answer the prayer." Thus the thousands of minor gods of Hinduism can be seen as the different faces of the universal spirit Brahman.

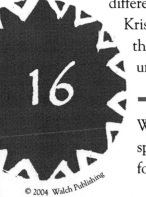

16

Which would you find easier to think about: Brahman as a formless universal spirit that is part of everything, or as a pantheon of different gods? Write three or four sentences for your answer.

Hinduism

Sri Ramakrishna

Sri Ramakrishna was a nineteenth-century Hindu sage. In his search for God, Ramakrishna faithfully followed the spiritual disciplines of several different religions. The following is an excerpt from one of Sri Ramakrishna's teachings on faith.

> God has made different religions to suit different aspirations, times, and countries. All doctrines are only so many paths; but a path is by no means God Himself. Indeed, one can reach God if one follows any of the paths with whole-hearted devotion. One may eat a cake with icing either straight or sidewise. It will taste sweet either way. . . . As one can ascend to the top of a house by means of a ladder or a bamboo or a staircase or a rope, so diverse are the ways and means to approach God, and every religion in the world shows one of these ways.

In your own words, explain what Sri Ramakrishna was saying here.

17

Hinduism

Hindu Gods

Hinduism has many gods. Three of them are **Brahma**, **Shiva**, and Vishnu. Brahma is known as the Creator. The universe and all creatures in it came from him. Vishnu is known as the Preserver. Associated with truth and righteousness, he maintains order. Shiva is the Destroyer. Shiva's destruction leads to good, as he removes impurity.

Although these three gods are sometimes called the Hindu Trinity, they are not of equal importance. Brahma's job—creation—is finished. The jobs of the other two gods remain.

18

Write two or three sentences about this view of the world in which the principles of creation, preservation, and destruction are connected. Which principle do you think is the most important one?

Hinduism

Gods and Symbolism

Statues and paintings of the Hindu gods are found in homes and temples throughout India. The different images of a particular god often have things in common. For example, Ganesha is usually shown with an elephant's head, and Shiva is often shown with three eyes. These images use symbolism to express the divine nature of the gods. Thus Ganesha's elephant head stands for wisdom. Shiva's left and right eyes indicate his activity in the physical world; the third eye symbolizes spiritual knowledge and power. For viewers familiar with the symbolism, each image conveys a great deal of information.

Symbols are used in many ways in different cultures. Think about how symbols are used in your daily life. Write two or three sentences to describe these symbols and what they stand for.

19

Shiva Nataraj

Shiva is one of the primary figures in Hinduism. He is often shown as *Shiva Nataraj*, or "Shiva, King of Dancers." Everything in this image has a meaning. Shiva is shown with four arms, one for each of the cardinal directions. He dances with his left foot raised. His right foot rests on a figure that represents illusion and ignorance. In his upper right hand he holds a drum that stands for the male-female principle. His lower right hand makes a gesture that means, "Be without fear." Snakes, which stand for the ego, are seen uncoiling from his arms, legs, and hair. The skull on his head stands for his conquest over death. He is placed within an arch of flames; these stand for the endless cycle of birth and death.

20

Shiva's right foot is on illusion and ignorance. What is the symbolism of this pose? Write one or two sentences for your answer.

Daily Warm-Ups: World Religions

Avatars of Vishnu

According to Hindu belief, whenever the order of the world is threatened, Vishnu the Preserver appears on Earth. He is often considered to have ten forms, or avatars, on Earth. First Vishnu appeared as a fish to rescue the world from a flood. Next, as a tortoise, he supported a mountain on his back. Third, as a boar, he killed a demon who had stolen the Vedas, or holy scriptures. In his fourth avatar, as half man, half lion, he killed a demon king who could not be harmed by man or beast. Next, as a dwarf, he tricked a demon king who had seized the universe. As the warrior Parashurama he destroyed a wicked king. As Rama, the perfect king, he killed the demon king Ravana. His eighth avatar was Krishna, the central character in the epic *Mahabharata*. Krishna's advice to another character became the beloved text Bhagavad Gita. Next Vishnu appeared as Buddha in order to remove suffering from the world. The tenth avatar of Vishnu, Kalki the Destroyer, has not yet appeared in the world. Kalki will wipe out the forces of evil.

21

Some people see a progression in the avatars of Vishnu. Look at these ten avatars. Describe any progression you see.

© 2004 Walch Publishing

Hinduism

What People Want

According to Hinduism, the things we want change as we go through life. At first, we want pleasure and worldly success. There is nothing wrong with wanting these things, as long as we act morally in seeking them. For example, we should not lie or cheat in order to gain success. We must achieve it honestly.

Some people may spend years seeking pleasure or striving for worldly success. We may even think that these things make us happy. Eventually, though, we find ourselves wanting more, because each of these goals is too narrow to satisfy our total nature.

22

Choose one of these goals to examine. Do you think it is too narrow to satisfy all aspects of human nature? Write two or three sentences for your answer.

Paths to Spirituality

One of the goals of Hinduism is to help people achieve their full spiritual potential. Since all people are different, Hinduism does not teach just one way to reach this goal. Instead it identifies four basic spiritual personality types and a path for each. These paths are known as *yoga*, which comes from the same root as the word *yoke*. It means "to place under training."

The first type includes people who seek spirituality through reflection. Their yoga is *jnana*, or knowledge. The second type includes people who seek to understand things emotionally. Their yoga is *bhakti*, devotion and love. The third type includes people who take an active approach to their goals. Their yoga is *karma*, or work. The fourth spiritual type includes people who like a methodical approach to understanding spirituality. Their path is *raja yoga*, or royal yoga. This is the yoga that uses physical postures to achieve spiritual illumination.

Daily Warm-Ups: World Religions

23

Think about yourself and your approach to things. Which of these approaches to spirituality would be best for you: jnana yoga, bhakti yoga, karma yoga, or raja yoga? Write one or two sentences explaining your answer.

Raja Yoga

Hinduism offers many paths to spirituality. One approach is called *raja yoga.* According to raja yoga, each of us has different layers of "self." The first layer is the physical self—our bodies. The second layer is the conscious part of our minds—the things we are aware of and try to think about. The third layer is the subconscious. This layer is shaped by our experiences, but we are usually not aware of how it affects us. The fourth layer is even deeper than the subconscious. It is the layer of Being.

24

The aim of raja yoga is to reach the layer of Being. The first step in reaching it calls for being completely still. Try doing this now. Sit for one minute without moving and without thinking. At the end of one minute, write your reactions to the first step of raja yoga.

Hinduism

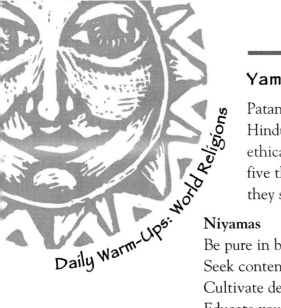

Yamas, Niyamas

Patanjali, an Indian sage who contributed to the development of Hinduism, lived around 200 B.C.E. Recognizing the need for a solid ethical foundation, Patanjali compiled an ethical code. It consists of five things people should do—the *niyamas*—and five ways in which they should exercise restraint—the *yamas*.

Niyamas
Be pure in body, mind, and speech.
Seek contentment.
Cultivate devotion.
Educate yourself.
Be steadfast in hardship.

Yamas
Practice nonviolence.
Discipline sexual desire.
Do not steal.
Do not lie.
Do not be greedy.

Patanjali compiled these precepts more than 2,000 years ago. Do you think they are relevant today? Write three or four sentences for your answer.

25

Hinduism

Guru

In Hinduism, those who wish to develop spiritually will listen to teachings. They may find a mentor called a guru. The word *guru* comes from two Sanskrit words, *gu* and *ru*. *Gu* means "darkness" or "ignorance." *Ru* means "remover" or "dispeller."

Based on the original meanings of the words *gu* and *ru*, write your own definition of the word *guru*.

26

Hinduism

Rig-Veda

The Rig-Veda ("Praising Knowledge"), composed around 1500 B.C.E., is the oldest of the Hindu scriptures. It is also the oldest book in any Indo-European language. It marks an early stage in the development of Hinduism.

A central story in the Rig-Veda tells of the god Indra and the dragon Vritra. Vritra had stolen all the water of the world for himself. Indra fights the dragon in order to take back the life-giving waters. After a monumental struggle, Indra defeats the dragon, and the waters are freed, bringing life to the land.

Daily Warm-Ups: World Religions

Explanations of this story often show Indra as a symbol for wind, Vritra as standing for clouds, and the waters as meaning the monsoon rains. Given what you know about India, why would the monsoon rains be a matter of life or death? Why might early Indians have seen the monsoon-bringing winds as a source of life? Write two or three sentences for your answer.

27

© 2004 Walch Publishing

Hinduism

The Ramayana

The Ramayana is one of India's national epics. It tells the story of Rama and his wife, Sita. Rama was the eldest son of the king of Ayodha. One of the king's wives wanted her son, Bharata, to be king. The king owed her two favors. She asked him to make Bharata his heir and to banish Rama for 14 years. Rama agreed to go, saying "I gladly obey my father's command." His wife, Sita, insisted on joining Rama in exile. She said, "Is not the wife's duty to be at her husband's side?"

Bharata tried to persuade Rama to return. Rama insisted on doing his duty, even after his father died. Bharata said he would rule in Rama's name; when the 14 years were up, Rama should become king.

During their exile, Sita was kidnapped, then rescued by Rama. After that, Rama and Sita returned to Ayodha, and Rama became king.

Rama, Sita, and Bharata are often held up as models of Hindu behavior. What did they do in this story that make them good role models? What does this tell you about Hindu ideals of behavior? Write two or three sentences for your answer.

The Bhagavad Gita and Mohandas Gandhi

The Bhagavad Gita, or "Song of God," is one of the most influential Hindu religious texts. It is part of the epic poem *Mahabharata*, which tells of a war between two sets of relatives. The Bhagavad Gita opens with Arjuna, the leader of one side, despairing at the thought of killing his kinsmen. His charioteer, Krishna—who later reveals himself as a god—urges him to do his duty as a noble by leading his men into battle. Krishna reassures Arjuna that our souls are immortal, so he cannot truly kill anyone. He then goes on to tell Arjuna of three ways that the soul can be freed from the cycle of death and rebirth. The soul can be freed through karma yoga, doing one's duty without self-interest in the consequences of one's actions; through jnana yoga, or withdrawal and concentration that lead to knowledge; and through bhakti yoga, or devotion to God.

Mohandas Gandhi led India's independence movement in the early twentieth century. He credited the Bhagavad Gita with helping him to cope with life's tragedies. Based on what you know of Mohandas Gandhi, write two or three sentences about the influence of the Bhagavad Gita on his life and work.

Daily Warm-Ups: World Religions

29

Hinduism

The *Bhagavad Gita*: The Eternal "This"

This is a quote from the *Bhagavad Gita*, one of the most influential Hindu religious texts. Read the excerpt. Then use your knowledge of Hinduism to explain what the text is saying.

> Know that to be imperishable whereby all this is pervaded. No one can destroy that immutable being. . . . This is never born nor ever dies, nor having been will ever not be any more; unborn, eternal, everlasting, ancient, this is not slain when the body is slain. . . . As a man casts off worn-out garments and takes others that are new, even so the embodied one casts off worn-out bodies and passes on to others new. This no weapons wound, this no fire burns, this no waters wet, this no wind doth dry. Beyond all cutting, burning, wetting and drying is this—eternal, all-pervading, stable, immovable, everlasting. Perceivable neither by the senses nor by the mind, this is called unchangeable; therefore knowing this as such thou shouldst not grieve.

30

Daily Warm-Ups: World Religions

Upanishads: The Chariot

The Upanishads are part of the Hindu scriptures. They include many metaphors and analogies. In one, a rider sits in a chariot, driven by a charioteer. The chariot represents the human body. The road the chariot travels on represents things that we perceive with our senses. The horses that pull the chariot represent the senses. The reins represent the mind, which controls the senses. The chariot driver represents the human mind or intuition. The owner of the chariot has full authority over the chariot, but does not need to do anything to direct it.

Daily Warm-Ups: World Religions

In this analogy, what do you think is represented by the owner of the chariot? Write one or two sentences for your answer.

Hinduism

The Yogi and the Scorpion

Many religions use teaching stories. This story is sometimes used to teach about Hinduism. Read the story. Then say what idea you think the story is trying to present.

A yogi was sitting by a river when he saw a scorpion fall into the water. The yogi scooped the scorpion up in his hand. The scorpion promptly stung him.

A minute later, the scorpion fell into the river again. Again, the yogi rescued it. And again, the scorpion stung the yogi.

For a third time, the scorpion fell into the river. And for a third time the yogi moved to rescue it. But another man had watched the whole thing, and stopped him. "Why do you keep rescuing the scorpion?" he asked. "The ungrateful creature keeps stinging you. Why don't you just let it drown?"

The yogi answered, "It is the nature of a scorpion to sting. It is the nature of a yogi to show compassion." And he scooped the scorpion out of the water again.

Hinduism

The Sage and the Snake

Many religions use stories in order to convey a particular moral belief. The following story is sometimes used to teach about Hinduism. Read it carefully. Then, in the space below, explain what you think the message of the story is.

A wandering sage arrived in a village. As he entered, he saw a huge, menacing snake. The villagers told the sage that the snake terrorized them and made their life difficult. The sage spoke to the snake and taught him about nonviolence, or *ahimsa*. The snake heard the sage's words and took them to heart.

The next year, the sage again came to the village. The once-magnificent snake was now thin and bruised. The sage said, "My friend, what has happened to you?" The snake replied, "Your words showed me the error of my ways, so I no longer acted with violence toward the village. Now they mock me. The children throw stones at me when I try to get food."

The sage looked at the snake, shaking his head. "My foolish friend," he said, "I told you not to bite the people. I never told you not to hiss."

33

© 2004 Walch Publishing

Hinduism

The Caste System

Indian society has traditionally been organized into groups called castes. People are born into the caste of their family. The caste system includes a strict hierarchy and rules for social interaction. Each caste also had certain rights and responsibilities.

Advocates of the caste system say that it is not discriminatory but makes life easier for members of all castes. According to them, the caste system just acknowledges that people are different. Some are natural administrators, some are better at working with their hands. Under the caste system, those who are good at routine work do not compete for jobs with strategic thinkers; they compete with their equals.

Opponents of the system say that this theory is fine, but in actuality, skills like leadership or manual dexterity are not hereditary traits. A person born in a low caste might be a gifted leader but would not be allowed to develop those gifts.

Based on your knowledge of people, do you think a system like the caste system would tend to level the playing field for all? Or would it tend to give certain people more privileges than others? Write three or four sentences for your answer.

34

Hinduism

A Multiplicity of Forms

We speak of Hinduism as one religion, which suggests that Hinduism is the same everywhere. This is not the case. India is a land of great variety. Even today, there are sixteen official languages in India and about 1,600 dialects. Geographically, rivers and mountains break the country into a number of distinct regions. The religion we call Hinduism developed over thousands of years, among hundreds of different groups of people. The religious traditions of all these different groups are included in Hinduism. Even today, Hinduism is changing. It is not one firm, fixed belief system, but a fluid system that includes many different beliefs.

How does an inclusive, ever-changing belief system compare to other major world belief systems? Choose another major world religion. Write three or four sentences comparing Hinduism and another religion.

35

Judaism

Facts About Judaism

Here are some facts about Judaism. Use them to write an informational paragraph about this ancient religion in the space below.

- 3,500 years old

- Founded by Abraham and Moses

- Monotheistic (a belief in one God)

- Jewish people are specially chosen by God.

- Followers worship in synagogues; their spiritual leaders are called rabbis.

- Has twelve million followers, most of whom are in Israel and the United States

- Six million Jews were murdered in the Holocaust in an attempt to wipe out Judaism.

36

Judaism

Biblical Phrases

Many everyday phrases were first used in the Bible. Draw a line from each biblical phrase to its meaning today.

Phrases

1. a drop in the bucket (Isaiah 40:15)

2. at their wits' end (Psalms 107:2)

3. a man after my own heart (I Samuel 13:14)

4. give up the ghost (Job 3:11)

5. as old as the hills (Job 15:7)

Meanings

a. unable to handle anything more

b. a kindred spirit

c. a small amount of a plentiful commodity

d. very, very old

e. to die, to cease working

37

Judaism

Jewish Names

Jewish history and culture have affected many aspects of Western civilization: its literature, its art, its philosophy. One small measure of this is the use of traditionally Jewish names. Abraham Lincoln was named for a Jewish patriarch. So was Noah Webster. Many people today have traditionally Jewish names, such as Adam, Luke, Joshua, Rachel, Sarah, Deborah, Naomi, and Nathan.

List as many well-known people as you can who carry Jewish names.

38

Judaism

Monotheism and Polytheism

Monotheism is a belief in one god alone. Polytheism is a belief in many gods. Around 2000 B.C.E., most peoples in the Mediterranean region believed in many gods. They saw each force of nature—the wind, the sun, the rain—as a separate deity. This was a way of explaining the world in which they lived.

Unlike most of their neighbors, the Jews believed in one god, not many. Think about what you know about the history and geography of the region. How do you think the Jewish belief in one god affected their interactions with other peoples? Write three or four sentences for your answer.

39

Judaism

Jewish History: Part 1

The history of the Jews goes back thousands of years. Below are some important events in the years before the Common Era (B.C.E.). Use your knowledge of Judaism and the history of the region to determine their correct order. Then number them 1–11, with 1 as the earliest event.

_____ a. Cyrus, king of Persia, allows the Jews to return to Judah.

_____ b. The kingdom of Israel splits in two. The northern kingdom continues to be called Israel. The southern kingdom is called Judah.

_____ c. Abraham, to whom the Jews trace their ancestry, is told to leave Mesopotamia and settle in Canaan, which is now Israel.

_____ d. When King Antiochus tries to force Jews to worship idols, a group of rebels overthrows the king.

_____ e. The kingdom of Israel is founded.

_____ f. Judah comes under the control of Alexander the Great.

_____ g. Moses leads the Israelites out of Egypt and receives the laws of God.

_____ h. The Babylonians conquer the southern kingdom of Judah.

_____ i. Persia conquers Babylonia.

_____ j. The Assyrians conquer the northern kingdom of Israel.

40

Judaism

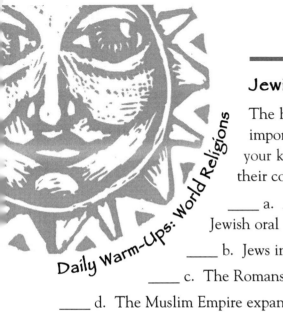

Daily Warm-Ups: World Religions

Jewish History: Part 2

The history of the Jews goes back thousands of years. Below are some important events in the first thousand years of the Common Era. Use your knowledge of Judaism and the history of the region to determine their correct order. Then number them 1–8, with 1 as the earliest event.

_____ a. After the Jewish expulsion from Jerusalem by the Romans, Jewish oral law is written down in a book called the Mishnah.

_____ b. Jews in the Roman Empire are repressed.

_____ c. The Romans reconquer Jerusalem and destroy the Temple.

_____ d. The Muslim Empire expands to cover southwestern Asia, northern Africa, and Spain.

_____ e. Jews rebel against Roman rule and seize Jerusalem.

_____ f. The Jews begin to scatter around the world.

_____ g. Christianity becomes the primary religion of the Roman Empire.

_____ h. The Romans crush the rebellion and prohibit Jews from living in Jerusalem.

41

Judaism

Jewish History: Part 3

The history of the Jews goes back thousands of years. Below are some important events in that history between 1000 and 1900. Use your knowledge of Judaism and the history of the region to determine their correct order. Then number them 1–8, with 1 as the earliest event.

_____ a. Jews from Eastern Europe begin to emigrate to Israel, then called Palestine.

_____ b. One hundred thousand Jews are massacred in Poland.

_____ c. The Crusades, intended to free the Holy Land from Muslim rule, begin; they result in the deaths of many Jews.

_____ d. A series of massacres of Jews, called pogroms, begins in Russia.

_____ e. Much of Europe blames the Black Plague on Jews; hundreds of Jewish communities destroyed.

_____ f. French Jews are granted full citizenship for the first time since the Roman Empire.

_____ g. Russia requires thirty-one years of military service for Jews, beginning at age twelve.

_____ h. Jews of Vienna are forced to move into a ghetto called Leopoldstadt.

42

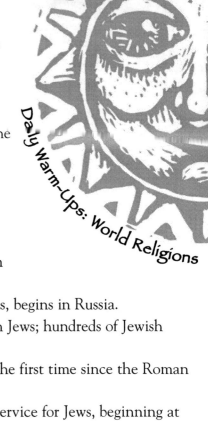

Daily Warm-Ups: World Religions

Judaism

The Jewish State of Israel

The history of the Jewish people and the history of the State of Israel are closely connected. Here are some important events in that history. Write the correct date or dates from the box on the line beside each event.

1916	1920s–1930s	1933	1939–1945
1948	1949	1950s–2000s	

_____ a. Armistice agreements are signed with Egypt, Jordan, Syria, Lebanon; Israel is admitted to the United Nations.

_____ b. Adolf Hitler comes to power in Germany.

_____ c. After World War I, France and Britain divide up the Middle East.

_____ d. Conflicts between Arabs and Jews continue.

_____ e. The State of Israel is declared; hostilities break out between Israelis and Arabs.

_____ f. The Holocaust results in the deaths of about six million Jews.

_____ g. With Palestine under British rule, Jewish immigration to Palestine increases.

43

Judaism

The Idol Seller

Abraham was a founder of Judaism. He was born around 1800 B.C.E. in the city of Ur. His father, Terah, made idols for people to worship. Abraham did not believe in idols; he believed in one god.

One day, Abraham was left to mind his father's store of idols. He smashed all the idols except one, then put the hammer in that idol's hands.

When Terah returned and saw the broken idols, he was furious. He shouted to Abraham, "What have you done? Why did you smash my idols?" Abraham replied that the idols had gotten into a fight, and the idol with the hammer had broken the other ones. Terah said, "What nonsense! I made these idols—they have no life or power, they can't do anything! You must have broken them!"

44

This answer gave Abraham the perfect argument to use with his father. What do you think Abraham said next? Write your answer here.

Judaism

The Empty Palace

Abraham was the first prophet of Judaism. According to the Midrash, a book of Jewish stories and aphorisms, Abraham was walking near the city of Ur when he saw an empty palace. For a moment he thought that the palace appeared before him like an illusion. Then he realized, of course, it was probably built by someone. In order for a palace to exist it must have been built. Likewise, Abraham reasoned that the world itself was made by something. This "something" is called God.

Do you think things can exist without having a beginning? Write a paragraph explaining your opinion.

45

© 2004 Walch Publishing

Judaism

The First Covenant

Abraham was the first prophet of Judaism. According to the Book of Genesis in the Bible, when Abraham was ninety-nine years old, the Lord appeared to him and made a covenant, or agreement, with him. God asked Abraham to do certain things. In return, he promised to take special care of Abraham's descendants and to give them the land of Israel.

Abraham is sometimes called the patriarch of the Jewish people. A patriarch is a father or founder. In what way was Abraham the patriarch of Judaism? Write two or three sentences for your answer.

Moses in the Basket

Around 1700 B.C.E., famine forced the Israelites to migrate to Egypt. Over time, the Israelites became like slaves in Egypt. Around 1200 B.C.E., the pharaoh, or ruler of Egypt, started to worry about the Israelites. He was afraid they might rebel against him. To keep them weak, he ordered that all boys born to the Israelites must be thrown into the river to drown.

One woman who had a son hid the baby as long as she could. When he was about three months old, she took a basket and made it as waterproof as she could. Then she put the baby in the basket and left him near the river's edge.

The daughter of the pharaoh found the basket. She guessed at once that the baby was an Israelite. But she was moved by pity for the baby. She arranged to have the baby nursed—by his own mother, though the princess didn't know this. Later she adopted the boy as her son. She named him Moses, which means "one who was drawn out," because, she said, "I drew him out of the water."

What kind of person do you think would try to rescue someone she didn't know and take him into her own home? Write two or three sentences for your answer.

Daily Warm-Ups: World Religions

47

Judaism

Moses and God

In the Book of Exodus in the Bible, Moses' first meeting with God is described. God tells Moses to call the Israelites together and to lead them out of Egypt. Moses answered:

> "But," objected Moses, "suppose they will not believe me, nor listen to my plea? For they may say, 'The Lord did not appear to you.'" (Exodus 4:1)

In response, God gave Moses a sign that would convince the Israelites that Moses had truly seen God.

If someone told you that he or she had seen God, would you believe them? What kind of sign would convince you? Write two or three sentences for your answer.

48

The Ten Plagues of Egypt

According to the Bible, God promised to deliver the Jews from slavery in Egypt. Directed by God, Moses asked the pharaoh to release the Jews. The pharaoh refused. God then sent ten plagues to the Egyptians; Jews were not affected by the plagues. First, the water in the Nile turned to blood. Then a wave of frogs covered the land. Next the dust of the earth was changed into gnats, which attacked people and animals. In the fourth plague, swarms of flies filled the air. Then came a disease that killed the Egyptians' livestock. Next the Egyptians suffered from painful boils. In the seventh plague, severe hail killed people and animals. Then came locusts, which ate any crops that survived the hail. The ninth plague brought three days of utter darkness, so that people could not see to move around. In the tenth plague, the firstborn sons in all Egyptian homes died. Finally, the pharaoh agreed to let the Jews leave Egypt.

The pharaoh refused to let the Jews leave until the tenth plague. How do you think ordinary Egyptians felt about this? Imagine living through plague after plague. Would you want to keep the Jews in Egypt, or let them go? Write two or three sentences explaining your answer.

49

Judaism

Passover

The Jews were freed from slavery in Egypt after God sent ten plagues to the Egyptians. In the last plague, the firstborn son of every house in Egypt died. Speaking through Moses, God directed the Jews to do certain things. Death would pass over the house of anyone who obeyed these directions. Jewish families were told to sacrifice a lamb and to mark their doors with its blood. They were then to roast the lamb, eating it with unleavened bread and bitter herbs. They were to dress as if they were traveling, with sandals on their feet and staffs in hand. God also told them that they should celebrate this event in the future by performing the same rite every year.

Moses explained, "When your children ask you, 'What does this rite of yours mean?' you shall reply, 'This is the Passover sacrifice of the Lord, who passed over the houses of the Israelites in Egypt; when he struck down the Egyptians, he spared our houses.'" (Exodus 12:26–27)

50

Passover is still celebrated in Jewish homes today, 3,000 years after the first Passover in Egypt. Why do you think this event is still celebrated? Write two or three sentences for your answer.

Judaism

Daily Warm-Ups: World Religions

The Commandments: A Moral Code

When Moses led the Jews out of Egypt, they crossed the Sinai Desert. God called Moses to the top of Mount Sinai and gave him the Ten Commandments. These commandments formed the moral code for the Jewish people. Some were injunctions—things the people were told to do. Some were prohibitions—things they were told not to do. Injunctions included keeping the Sabbath day holy and honoring one's parents. Prohibitions included worshipping other gods, making idols, taking God's name in vain, killing, committing adultery, theft, bearing false witness, and wanting things that belong to other people.

Do you think these ten commandments are a good foundation for a code of conduct? Write two or three sentences to explain your answer.

51

Judaism

The Commandments: A Legal Code

The Ten Commandments combine religious and moral rules in a code for Jewish people. Many of the moral rules are now enforced by laws. Read the commandments. Then circle those that are addressed today by laws in the United States.

1. You shall have no other gods but me.

2. You shall not make any idols.

3. You shall not take the name of your Lord in vain.

4. You shall remember and keep holy the Sabbath day.

    5. Honor your father and mother.

    6. You shall not kill.

    7. You shall not commit adultery.

    8. You shall not steal.

    9. You shall not bear false witness against your neighbor.

    10. You shall not covet your neighbor's goods.

Daily Warm-Ups: World Religions

Daily Warm-Ups: World Religions

Judaism

The Meaning of the Commandments

The Ten Commandments, the moral code for the Jewish people, are short and to the point. But each one carries a great deal of meaning. Read the commandments carefully. Then choose one commandment. Explain—in detail—what it means and how it can apply to people's lives.

1. You shall have no other gods but me.

2. You shall not make any idols.

3. You shall not take the name of your Lord in vain.

4. You shall remember and keep holy the Sabbath day.

5. Honor your father and mother.

6. You shall not kill.

7. You shall not commit adultery.

8. You shall not steal.

9. You shall not bear false witness against your neighbor.

10. You shall not covet your neighbor's goods.

53

© 2004 Walch Publishing

Judaism

Tanakh: Hebrew Scriptures

The name for the collected Hebrew scriptures is Tanakh. This name comes from the Hebrew letters for the three parts of the scriptures: *Torah, Nevi'im,* and *Ketuvim.*

Torah, which means "Teaching," includes the books of Genesis, Exodus, Leviticus, Numbers, and Deuteronomy. Nevi'im, which means "Prophets," includes the books of Joshua, Judges, I Samuel, II Samuel, I Kings, II Kings, Isaiah, Jeremiah, Ezekiel, Hosea, Joel, Amos, Obadiah, Jonah, Micah, Nahum, Habakkuk, Zephaniah, Haggai, Zechariah, and Malachi. Ketuvim, which means "Writings," includes the books of Psalms, Proverbs, Job, Song of Songs, Ruth, Lamentations, Ecclesiastes, Esther, Daniel, Ezra, Nehemiah, I Chronicles, and II Chronicles.

54

Write the part of Tanakh each of the following books is found in.

1. Isaiah _____

2. Leviticus _____

3. Daniel _____

4. Proverbs _____

Judaism

David and Goliath

Around 1100 B.C.E., the Jews were in conflict with a tribe called the Philistines. Both sides chose a champion to fight in a single combat. The champion of the Philistines was a giant named Goliath. An Israelite shepherd named David came to the battlefield to deliver bread to his brothers, who were soldiers. When David heard Goliath speaking to the Israelites, he volunteered to be the champion of his people. Goliath went into battle fully armed, carrying great weapons. The Israelites tried to give David arms and armor, but he was unused to carrying so much weight. Instead he put five smooth stones in his pocket, along with the sling he used to protect his sheep.

The two combatants looked ill-matched: one a giant in bronze armor, one a slight young man, unarmed.

But as the Philistine moved forward to meet David, the shepherd put a stone in his sling, hurled it, and struck the giant in the forehead. Goliath fell to the ground. The Philistines, shocked at the death of their champion, fled.

This story is the origin of the phrase "like David and Goliath." What do you think this phrase means? Explain it in your own words.

55

© 2004 Walch Publishing

The Book of Isaiah

Prophets are people who have a special ability for listening to and speaking for God. The prophet Isaiah, who lived around the eighth century B.C.E., was an adviser to the king of Judah. At that time, the kingdom was under attack from Assyria. Isaiah told the king that God would protect the people if they had faith, but if they rejected God, they would be destroyed.

> My friend had a vineyard on a fertile hillside; he spaded it, cleared it of stones, and planted the choicest vines; . . . Then he looked for the crop of grapes, but what it yielded was wild grapes. . . . Now, I will let you know what I mean to do to my vineyard:
> Take away its hedge, give it to grazing, break through its wall, let it be trampled! Yes, I will make it a ruin: it shall not be pruned or hoed, but overgrown with thorns and briers; I will command the clouds not to send rain upon it. The vineyard of the Lord of hosts is the house of Israel, and the men of Judah are his cherished plant. (Isaiah 5:1–7)

56

In your own words, explain what Isaiah was saying here.

Daily Warm-Ups: World Religions

A Light Unto the Nations

The prophet Isaiah said to the Jewish people, "Be a light unto the nations." This is one of the responsibilities of being a Jew. To do this, Jews are directed to study and live by the laws of Moses. These laws are the very will of God.

What do you think it means to be a "light" to other nations? Describe someone or something that is a "light" to you.

57

The Maccabean Revolt

Around 333 B.C.E., Alexander the Great conquered Israel. However, the Jews were allowed to continue practicing their own religion.

This ended in 175 B.C.E. when Antiochus IV became king. Antiochus wanted to make Jerusalem a Greek city. He banned Jewish Sabbath observance and scripture study. He built an altar to Zeus in the temple and forced Jews to make sacrifices to Greek gods.

Many Jews accepted the Greek religion in order to maintain peace. But some didn't. Finally, in 167 B.C.E., a revolt broke out. It was led by Judah Maccabee, son of a priest. Most of the Jewish fighters were farmers, not soldiers. Still, they managed to defeat the Greek army and liberate Jerusalem in 165 B.C.E.

Judah and his followers reconsecrated the temple. The final step was lighting the lamp in the temple. A special oil was used for this lamp; it took several days to prepare properly. When they went to light the lamp, they found only enough oil for one day. Still, they filled the lamp and lit it. Amazingly, the lamp continued to burn. It burned for eight days—long enough for more oil to be prepared.

This event is still celebrated today in a celebration sometimes known as the Festival of Lights. What is the proper name of this festival?

58

Daily Warm-Ups: World Religions

Judaism

Hillel and the Meaning of Torah

Hillel was a Jewish teacher who lived around 70 B.C.E. He was devoted to the study of Torah, or Jewish sacred writings. One day a non-Jew came to Hillel intending to mock Torah. He said to Hillel, "Teach me the Torah in the time I can balance on one foot. If you do this, I will convert to Judaism." Hillel responded, "The main idea of the Torah is 'What is hateful to you, do not do to your neighbor.' Everything else is commentary."

The visitor was so impressed with Hillel's response that he began to study Torah seriously and became a Jew.

What is your reaction to Hillel's response? Write two or three sentences for your answer.

59

Daily Warm-Ups: World Religions

Judaism

The Fall of Masada

Masada is an oblong mountain in Israel, near the Dead Sea. It has steep sides but an almost flat top and a panoramic view of the land around it.

In 70 C.E., Jerusalem was conquered by a Roman army, and the temple was destroyed. A group of about 1,000 Jewish resisters, called Zealots, fled Jerusalem and went to Masada. A fortress stood at the top of the mountain. Surrounded by ravines, the fortress was approached only by two narrow tracks. The Zealots took refuge in this inaccessible place.

The 15,000-man Roman army laid siege to Masada. Because of the mountain's steep sides, they could not come close enough to the fortress to take it. Finally after a two-year siege, the Romans managed to build a ramp up one of the slopes of the mountain. When they entered the fortress, they found the Zealots dead. Rather than surrender to the Romans, the Zealots had killed themselves. Only seven women and children, who had hidden in a cistern, remained alive to surrender.

Today Masada is a symbol of freedom and independence for the Jews. Why do you think this is so? Write two or three sentences in explanation.

Judaism

The Mishnah

By 200 C.E., Jews had developed an extensive set of laws that dealt with everything from daily prayer to the judicial system to taxation. These laws were passed on orally, not in writing, because any written version was necessarily incomplete and thus subject to misinterpretation.

However, after the Jewish rebellion in 132 C.E., the Roman rulers prohibited Jews from living in Jerusalem. Jewish leaders realized that their expulsion from Jerusalem could leave them without teachers or temple to maintain this oral tradition. To keep the laws from being lost, they decided to write them down. In around 200 C.E., Rabbi Judah Ha-Nasi prepared the first written version, the Mishnah.

What are the advantages of having a teaching in written form? What are the disadvantages? What can teachers do that books cannot? Write two or three sentences for your answer.

61

Judaism

The Talmud

By the year 500 C.E., all existing Jewish holy books were gathered into one book called the Talmud. This book contains all the Jewish laws and the essential stories and aphorisms of Judaism. To study, understand, and carry out the teachings in the Talmud is one way to be a practicing Jew.

Some people think of laws as things that restrict their actions. Others see laws as creating a framework within which to act. How do you think having a clear system of laws can be helpful? Write down as many ideas as you can.

62

Judaism

Maimonides and Nachmanides

Around the end of the 600s, Spain's Christian rulers outlawed Judaism. Then, in 711, the Moors invaded, and Spain became part of a vast Islamic empire. Under Moorish rule, Spain became a center of Jewish learning and culture, with Jewish poets, philosophers, and statesmen. This period was known as the Jewish Golden Age in Spain.

Two thinkers of this period were Moses Maimonides (1135–1204) and Moses ben Nachman (1194–1270).

Moses Maimonides was born in Spain and moved to Cairo in 1165. In Egypt, he spent a great deal of time studying the Talmud. Maimonides focused on the human intellect. He wrote about the importance of studying, the "work of the mind."

Moses ben Nachman—also known as Nachmanides—spent most of his life in Spain, moving to Israel just a few years before his death. Like Maimonides, Nachmanides was both a physician and a Talmud scholar. However, Nachmanides wrote that the human soul and spirit were more important than intellect and studying.

Which is more important to you, the intellect or spirit? Explain your opinion in two or three sentences.

63

Taoism

The Way of Tao

Taoism is one of the traditional religions of China. The word *Tao* (pronounced "dow") means "way" or "path." The "way" of Taoism is the way of the universe. Taoism advocates living simply and not interfering with the course of natural events.

In what ways do people often interfere with the course of natural events? List as many ways as you can. What is the effect of this interference?

64

Taoism

Lao Tzu

The legendary founder of Taoism was a philosopher named Lao Tzu who lived in China around 600 B.C.E. (His name is also sometimes spelled Laotse.) One story about Lao Tzu says that Confucius, another Chinese philosopher, once visited him. Asked about the visit, Confucius said:

> Of birds I know they have wings to fly with,
>
> of fish they have fins to swim with,
>
> of wild beasts that they have feet to run with.
>
> For feet there are traps, for fins nets, for wings arrows.
>
> But who knows how dragons surmount wind and clouds into heaven ?
>
> This day I have seen Lao Tzu and he is a dragon.

What do you think Confucius meant by this? Explain it in your own words.

65

The Tao Te Ching

When he was 160, Lao Tzu, the founder of Taoism, left China so that he could pursue a natural life somewhere else. He mounted a water buffalo and rode toward the boundaries of China. A warden at the boundary had dreamed that a sage would come. When Lao Tzu arrived, he recognized him as the sage from his dream. The warden begged him to write down the principles of his philosophy. Lao Tzu sat down and composed the Tao Te Ching (pronounced "dow dir jing"). He then remounted his water buffalo and rode off. No one ever heard of him again. Translated as "The Way and its Power," the Tao Te Ching is the central scripture of Taoism.

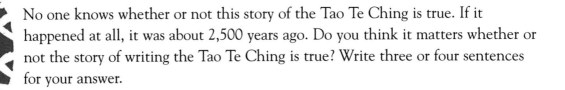

66

No one knows whether or not this story of the Tao Te Ching is true. If it happened at all, it was about 2,500 years ago. Do you think it matters whether or not the story of writing the Tao Te Ching is true? Write three or four sentences for your answer.

Lao Tzu as Founder

The philosopher Lao Tzu is considered the founder of Taoism. Nobody is sure, though, whether or not he actually existed. We don't even know what his real name was; *Lao Tzu* means "The Old Man" or "The Grand Old Master." Lao Tzu didn't try to organize a religion. He didn't preach. He only wrote his ideas down because a border patrolman asked him to. Having written the Tao Te Ching, the central scripture of Taoism, Lao Tzu rode off and was never heard of again.

Does this description fit with your idea of the type of person who would found a religion? Why or why not? Write three or four sentences for your answer.

Taoism

The Authentic Life

According to the philosopher Lao Tzu, the founder of Taoism, most people do not live an authentic life. They live in a way that society suggests they live. People tend not to do things for themselves or to find out what they truly want. Instead they often do the things others want them to do.

What does it mean to be authentic? What would it mean to live an authentic life? Write two or three sentences for your answer.

68

A Single Step

The Chinese philosopher Lao Tzu, the founder of Taoism, is credited with saying, "A journey of a thousand miles begins with a single step."

What does this mean? Rewrite this saying in your own words.

69

The Tao of Ultimate Reality

In Taoism, the Tao, or Way, can be understood in many ways. First, the Tao is the way of ultimate reality. It is the ground of all existence, but it goes beyond the senses and words. The first lines of the Tao Te Ching, the scripture of Taoism, state this:

> The Tao that can be followed is not the eternal Tao.
>
> The name that can be named is not the eternal name.

In your own words, explain these lines.

70

Taoism

The Tao of the Universe

In Taoism, the Tao, or Way, can be understood in many ways. One meaning of the Tao is that it is the way of the universe.

> The universe lasts forever.
>
> Why does the universe last forever?
>
> It is unborn,
>
> So ever living.

Many aspects of the universe—such as our water cycle—are cyclical, always beginning, always ending. Choose some aspect of the universe. Explain it in terms of an unending cycle.

71

Taoism

The Tao of Daily Life

In Taoism, the Tao, or Way, can be understood in many ways. One meaning of the Tao is that it is the way people should live their daily lives. Instead of struggling with nature, we should adapt ourselves to nature.

List as many ways as you can in which people try to adapt nature to our use, instead of adapting ourselves to nature.

72

Taoism

Going With the Flow

Many religions use stories as a way of teaching people how to live. Here is a Taoist story. Read it carefully. Then, in the space below, explain what you think the message of the story is.

An old man was walking with friends by a swift-flowing river when he stumbled and fell into the water. He was swept downstream through a set of fierce rapids, dashing among the rocks. Then he plunged over the edge of a steep waterfall. His friends, fearing for his life, ran to the pool below the waterfall. To their amazement the old man came to the edge of the pool, unharmed.

"Old man," they cried, "how could you have survived both the rapids and the waterfall?"

"I cannot tell you," he answered. "I only know that I did not try to fight the water, but allowed myself to be shaped by it. I accommodated myself to the stream, and the stream carried me without harm."

73

Daily Warm-Ups: World Religions

Taoism

Wu Wei

Wu Wei (pronounced "woo-way") is an important principle in Taoism. *Wu wei* is the process by which we can come closer to the Tao, or Way. It has been described as "action through inaction" or "creative quietude." It does not mean that we do nothing and wait for things to fall into our laps. Rather, it means studying life so that we can accomplish things through minimal action. We can see this in action in martial arts such as judo, where defense consists of using an attacker's own force against him or her, rather than fighting against it.

Water is often described as having the virtues of *wu wei*. Think about water in different forms: as a steady drip, as a river, as a waterfall. How does it show the virtues of "action through inaction"? Write two or three sentences for your answer.

74

Taoism

Wu Wei: Action in Inaction

Wu wei, or "action through inaction," can be used in many ways. For example, if someone treats us with anger or with hatred, we should not respond in the same way. This will just make things worse. A Taoist story shows this principle at work. Read the story carefully. Then answer the question that follows.

There was once a great warrior who, though old, had never been beaten. One day a young warrior challenged him. The young man was not only strong, he was skilled at spotting any weakness in an opponent. He would let the opponent make the first move, thus revealing his weakness. Then the young warrior would strike and defeat his opponent.

The old warrior accepted the challenge and the two stood facing each other, prepared for battle. For a long time, neither man moved. Then to provoke the old man, the young man began hurling insults at him. He threw dirt at him and spat in his face. But the old warrior merely stood there. Unable to provoke the old warrior into showing any weakness, the young warrior finally acknowledged that he was beaten.

How did the old man use *wu wei* in this fight? Explain.

75

© 2004 Walch Publishing

Wu Wei in Your Life

A person who lives according to the Taoist principle of *wu wei*, or "action through inaction," is able to achieve things without strain. *Wu wei* is like floating in saltwater: if we give ourselves up to the water, we can achieve our goal—floating—without effort. But if we fight against the natural action of the water—for example, by trying to dive deep—we have to struggle to achieve our goal.

Think of a time when you acted in accord with *wu wei*, achieving your goal without strain. Write two or three sentences to describe it.

76

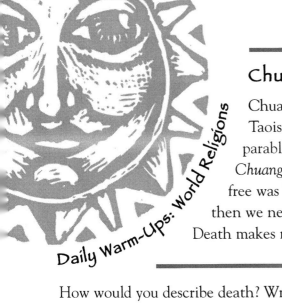

Taoism

Chuang Tzu and Death

Chuang Tzu, who lived from about 369 to 268 B.C.E., was a leading Taoist thinker. (His name is also sometimes spelled Chuangtse.) His parables and anecdotes were collected in a book that bears his name, *Chuang-tzu*. Chuang Tzu said that the only way to be happy and truly free was by understanding the Tao, or Way. If we understand the Way, then we need not fear death, as it is merely an inevitable part of the Way. Death makes new life possible.

How would you describe death? Write two or three sentences in explanation.

77

Taoism

Chuang Tzu and Skill

Chuang Tzu, a leading Taoist teacher, wrote about the pleasure and importance of skill. It is possible to slip into a kind of meditative state where one can perform effortlessly at painting, singing, dancing, and so forth.

We've all had experiences like this, where something suddenly seems effortless. When have you had an experience like this? What were you doing? How did the experience affect your sense of time? Write three or four sentences to describe the experience.

78

Taoism

Dreams

Chuang Tzu was a leading Taoist thinker. His teachings are collected in a book, *Chuang-tzu*. This story appears in *Chuang-tzu*. Read it carefully. Then write one or two sentences explaining what you think it means in the space below.

Once upon a time, I, Chuang Tzu, dreamt I was a butterfly, fluttering hither and thither, to all intents and purposes a butterfly. I was conscious only of my happiness as a butterfly, unaware that I was Tzu. Soon I awoke, and there I was, veritably myself again. Now I do not know whether I was then a man dreaming I was a butterfly, or whether I am now a butterfly, dreaming I am a man.

79

Taoism

Fish Story

The Taoist teacher Chuang Tzu was walking with a friend over a bridge. Chuang Tzu saw some fish darting about and said, "That is happiness for a fish."

His friend said, "You're not a fish! How do you know what makes a fish happy?"

Chuang Tzu responded, "You're not me! How do you know I don't know what makes a fish happy?"

80

What was Chuang Tzu saying to his friend? Write two or three sentences for your answer.

Taoism

On Politics

Chuang Tzu, the Taoist thinker, was offered a job at the emperor's court. He responded:

> Sir, have you seen a sacrificial ox? It is decked in fine garments and fed on fresh grass and beans. However, when it is led into the Great Temple, even though it might earnestly wish to be a simple calf again, it's now impossible.

What do you think Chuang Tzu meant by this? Write two or three sentences for your answer.

81

Taoism

Understanding the Universe

The Taoist thinker Chuang Tzu lived about 2,500 years ago, at a time when people knew very little about the world around them. Still he tried to understand the phenomena of nature. He wrote:

> Do the heaven's revolve? Does the earth stand still? Do the sun and the moon contend for their positions? Who has the time to keep them all moving? Is there some mechanical device that keeps them going automatically? Or do they merely continue to revolve, inevitably, of their own inertia?

> Do the clouds make rain? Or is it the rain that makes the clouds? What makes it descend so copiously? Who is it that has the leisure to devote himself, with such abandoned glee, to making these things happen?

Given what you know about Taoism, why do you think Chuang Tzu might have been interested in the workings of nature? Write two or three sentences for your answer.

Taoism

In Front of the Chariot

The Taoist teacher Chuang Tzu often used stories to present important ideas. Here is one of these stories.

> A praying mantis was standing in the road when a chariot came along. The insect thought he could stop the chariot by waving it away. But the charioteer did not even see the mantis, and it was crushed.

The Taoist lesson is that it is important to know when you can affect events and when you can't.

Write two or three sentences about a time when you stepped in front of a "charging chariot." When did you think you could affect something when you were actually powerless?

83

Taoism

Yin and Yang

The concept of balance is important in Taoism. Everything in the universe is a balance of opposite forces. Night is balanced by day; summer is balanced by winter. Often the opposite is necessary for completion. For example, a cup holds liquid because it has solid sides, but it also needs a hollow center to function. If the entire cup were solid, we couldn't put liquid into it. The cup must be both substance and space.

Taoism refers to these opposing, balancing elements of the universe as *yin* and *yang*. Yin is associated with darkness, yang with light. These are not aspects of good and bad, though; they are merely two sides of the same thing.

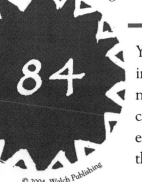

84

You can use your own breathing to experiment with yin and yang. We need air in our lungs in order to live. But to take air in, we need to push air out. We need empty lungs before we can fill them. Take a deep breath; fill your lungs completely. Hold the breath for a moment. Now try to breathe in without first emptying your lungs. What happened? Write two or three sentences to describe the experience.

Taoism

The Yin-Yang Symbol

The yin-yang symbol shows the opposite, balanced forces of the universe important in Taoism. Yin and yang are in tension, but they are not in opposition to each other. When both yin and yang are equally present, all is calm. When one is outweighed by the other, there is confusion.

Even in this symbol, the dark, yin side has a spot of white. The light, yang side has a spot of black. According to Taoism, nothing is absolutely dark or bright, good or bad. Everything contains both yang and yin.

Do you think this symbol conveys the idea of opposite, but balanced, forces? Write two or three sentences for your answer.

85

Taoism

Yin and Yang: Opposites or Pairs?

There are many ways of looking at the Taoist idea of yin and yang. Instead of thinking about characteristics like light and dark as opposites, it is better to think of them as pairs. Light and dark are a pair that belongs together. They help to define each other.

Think about the opposite sensations of heat and cold. Write a paragraph about heat depending on cold for its identity.

86

Taoism

The Energy of Qi

According to Taoism, things such as water, food, and sleep are necessary for life. Life itself, though, is a breathlike force called *qi* (pronounced "chee"). Qi is the energy that flows through the universe and all living things.

Do you think there is an energy in all living things? Write two or three sentences for your answer.

87

© 2004 Walch Publishing

Taoism

Qi and Balance

In traditional Chinese medicine, it is believed that disease is caused by an imbalance of *qi*, or living energy. Like a steady river, qi needs to flow and circulate evenly in the body. Qi does not flow when there are blockages or drains. To heal a patient, doctors of traditional Chinese medicine correct the flow by touching points on the body where qi is generated.

Does this explanation of health make sense to you? Write two or three sentences for your answer.

88

People, Nature, Tao

The Tao Te Ching, the first book of Taoism, says that humankind follows the earth, the earth follows nature, and nature follows the Tao.

In what ways does humankind follow the earth? Do we also fail to follow it? Write two or three sentences for your answer.

89

Buddhism

Siddhartha Gautama, the Buddha

Siddhartha Gautama, the founder of Buddhism, was born in Nepal in about 563 B.C.E. He was the son of a king, When Siddhartha was born, his father was told that the boy had two possible futures. He would be either a great king or a great spiritual leader.

Siddhartha's father wanted him to be a king. He gave Siddhartha every luxury and kept him from any sadness. Then a series of carriage rides changed Siddhartha's life. On the first ride, he saw an old person for the first time. He had not known that old age existed. On the next ride, he saw a sick person. He became aware of sickness and disease. Next he saw a corpse, and became aware of death. Finally he saw a holy man who had given up the world for the sake of spiritual things. Siddhartha decided that he, too, would give up the life he knew in order to seek spiritual fulfillment.

90

Why do you think that seeing old age, sickness, and death prompted Siddhartha to leave his life as a prince?

Buddhism

A Life-Changing Incident

Siddhartha Gautama was raised as a prince. Then a series of carriage rides changed his life. He left his home to search for spiritual fulfillment. He eventually found enlightenment, becoming the Buddha, the Awakened One, and the founder of Buddhism.

Think of an event or experience that changed your world. (It doesn't need to be as complete or as sudden as the change Siddhartha experienced.) Describe the experience and how it affected you.

91

Buddhism

"I Am Awake."

After his enlightenment, the Buddha passed a man on the road. This man saw that the Buddha was different from other men.

He asked the Buddha "Are you a god?"

The Buddha replied "No."

The man continued, "Then are you a magician or a wizard?"

"No."

"Are you a man?"

"No."

"Then what are you?" said the man.

The Buddha answered "I am awake."

Thus he was given his name. *Buddha* means "The Awakened One."

92

What do you think the Buddha meant by this answer? Write two or three sentences in explanation.

Buddhism

Terms in Buddhism

All religions have terms with special meanings. Here are some terms used in Buddhism. Some of these terms have been adopted into English. However, some have different meanings in English. Draw a line from each term to the best definition of its meaning.

1. bodhisattva

2. buddha

3. dharma

4. enlightenment

5. samsara

a. a person who is ready to enter nirvana

b. the realization of one's true nature and the nature of everything in the universe

c. an enlightened person who tries to help others attain enlightenment

d. the cycle of birth and death

e. a teaching of the Buddha

93

Buddhism

Buddha Speaks

The Buddha is the founder of Buddhism. He said:

> Do not accept anything on mere hearsay (i.e., thinking that thus have
> we heard it from a long time). Do not accept by mere tradition (i.e.,
> thinking that it has thus been handed down through many generations).
> Do not accept anything on account of rumors (i.e., by believing what others
> say without any investigation). Do not accept anything just because it accords
> with your scriptures. Do not accept anything by mere supposition. Do not
> accept anything by mere inference. Do not accept anything merely considering
> their appearances. Do not accept anything merely because it agrees to your
> preconceived notions. Do not accept anything merely because it seems acceptable
> (i.e., should be accepted). Do not accept anything thinking that the ascetic is respected by us
> (and therefore it is right to accept his word).

94

What do you think the Buddha meant by this? Summarize it in your own words.

Buddhism

Enlightenment

When Siddhartha became fully enlightened, he realized that people are not really separate from each other; we are all interconnected. He also realized that nothing in life is permanent; things change. Suffering is always a part of life, but there is a path that leads away from suffering.

In Buddhism, *enlightenment* means reaching a state beyond desire and suffering. But the word also has other meanings. Write two or three sentences about the meanings of the word *enlightenment*.

95

Buddhism

Taking Refuge

People who listen and accept the teachings of the Buddha are said to "take refuge." This means they go to the Buddha (the Enlightened One), *dharma* (the teachings of Buddha), and the *sangha* (those who follow the Buddha) for protection.

There are many challenges in life. What do you need refuge from? To whom or what do you go for protection? Write two or three sentences for your answer.

96

Buddhism

The Four Noble Truths

The Four Noble Truths are central to Buddhism. These truths were taught by the Buddha shortly after he became enlightened. The First Noble Truth is that life is frustrating and full of suffering, or *dukkha*. The Second Noble Truth is that suffering is caused by *tanha*, the desire for private fulfillment. The Third Noble Truth is that suffering can come to an end. If suffering is caused by selfish desire, it can be cured by overcoming desire. The Fourth Noble Truth is that there is a path that leads away from suffering, the Eightfold Path. This path consists of eight practices that the Buddha believed would lead to enlightenment.

How could these four ideas form the core of a way of life? Write three or four sentences in explanation.

97

Buddhism

The Eightfold Path

The Buddha devised the Eightfold Path to help others free themselves from suffering. The path calls for eight practices: Right Views, Right Intent, Right Speech, Right Conduct, Right Work, Right Effort, Right Mindfulness, and Right Concentration.

Think about what each of these practices might mean. How could they be applied? Choose one practice. Write two or three sentences explaining how you could apply it in your life.

98

Buddhism

Right Views

The first step on the Eightfold Path of Buddhism is called *Right Views*. This step means that you see clearly what is wrong with life. It also means that you understand the Four Noble Truths: we suffer by grasping at things we do not need and running from things that we need not fear, but we can be freed from suffering if we follow the Eightfold Path.

Do you grasp at things you do not need? Are there things you fear for no reason? Write two or three sentences about them.

99

Buddhism

Right Intent

The second step on the Eightfold Path of Buddhism is called *Right Intent*. This has to do with willingness. It is not enough to understand the Four Noble Truths. We must be willing to base our actions on them. Sometimes we know something is good for us but we don't do it, or we continue to do something we know is bad for us.

We all have things we know we should be doing, but we don't do. They can be small things, like taking vitamins. They can be big things, like preparing ourselves for life after school. Choose something you know you should be doing, but don't do. Think about why you don't do it. Then write two or three sentences explaining what it is and why you don't do it.

100

Buddhism

Right Speech

The third step on the Eightfold Path of Buddhism is called *Right Speech*. According to Buddhism, we are not aware of our own speech, but the way we speak can affect our behavior. Buddhism asks people to avoid lies, slander, harsh words, and frivolous speech.

What effect do these things have on other people? Describe a time when you heard someone lying or using harsh words. How did it affect you?

101

Buddhism

Right Conduct

Right Conduct is the fourth step on the Eightfold Path of Buddhism. It asks people not to kill, steal, or commit sexual misconduct. According to Buddhists, every action creates a karma. Karmas are like seeds; a small action will grow into something large. If that action is bad, the result will be bad. It is important, therefore, to avoid bad actions.

Have you ever seen or read about someone who acted in a bad way and had it lead to a bad result? Could the bad action have been avoided? Describe what happened in two or three sentences.

102

Buddhism

Right Work

Right Work is the fifth step on the Eightfold Path of Buddhism. This step encourages people to earn a living from a morally sound job. The way you make a living should not conflict with your spiritual progress.

What kinds of jobs do you think would conflict with spiritual progress? Why? What jobs would fit in with making spiritual progress? Why? List as many of both as you can think of.

103

Buddhism

Right Effort

Right Effort is the sixth step on the Eightfold Path of Buddhism.
Right Effort means applying yourself diligently in everything you
do. Sometimes we perform tasks halfheartedly because we don't like
them or we're in a hurry. Right Effort asks people to give every
action their full attention and effort.

To what do you apply yourself fully? Why do these things receive your
complete attention and effort?

104

Buddhism

Right Mindfulness

Right Mindfulness is the seventh step on the Eightfold Path. According to Buddhism, the mind is very powerful. It can affect every part of our lives. However, most of us pass the day in an unmindful state. We are not aware of what we do or of what happens around us.

Spend a few minutes practicing mindfulness. Look around you. Write down everything you see. Listen closely. What sounds can you distinguish? Write them down. Now listen to yourself. What thoughts pass through your head? Write them down, too.

105

Buddhism

Right Concentration

The final step of the Eightfold Path of Buddhism is *Right Concentration*. Have you ever looked through an unfocused camera or microscope? Everything is blurred. Focusing the lens makes a difference in what can be seen; the image becomes sharp and clear. This is similar to the difference Right Concentration can make. It helps you to see things as they really are, instead of a blurred version.

Most of us find it easy to focus on some things, but hard to focus on others. Still, we can practice focusing so that it becomes easier. What are you able to focus on easily? What things are harder for you to focus on? List them here. Why do you think it is harder for you to focus on some things more than others? What can you do to change this?

106

Buddhism

Right Association

The Buddha stressed the importance of right association. He said that people cannot find the truth unless the people they spend time with also seek the truth.

Think of a situation where a person's decisions are affected by the people around them. This could be a real situation or something you make up. Describe it in two or three sentences.

107

Buddhism

Death of the Buddha

The Buddha died in about 183 B.C.E. He had gone from a prince to an ascetic, from a wealthy man to a nomadic beggar. For more than fifty years he wandered India, teaching others about enlightenment.

Imagine that you are a newspaper columnist. Write an obituary for the Buddha as if for a modern newspaper. Include as much information as you can about the people who were important in his life and the events that shaped his life and beliefs.

108

Buddhism

The Buddha and Traditional Religion

Scholar Huston Smith has identified six common aspects of traditional religion. They are authority, ritual, speculation (answers to questions like "Why are we here?"), tradition, grace, and mystery. But these aspects are not found in Buddhism. Imagine a conversation between the Buddha and a student, where the Buddha is asked about one of these aspects of religion. What do you think the Buddha would have said? Write a short dialogue to show the conversation.

Buddhism

The Diamond Sutra

The oldest printed book in the world was printed in China around 868 C.E. It is a copy of the *Diamond Sutra,* one of the teachings of the Buddha. The sutra ends with these lines:

> Think of this fleeting world
>
> As a star at dawn, a bubble in a stream;
>
> A flash of lightning in a summer cloud,
>
> A flickering lamp, a phantom, and a dream.

110

What do you think the Buddha meant by this? Write two or three sentences in explanation.

Buddhism

Sunyata

According to Buddhism, things don't have an essence that defines them. This idea is called *sunyata,* or emptiness. For example, you know what a car is, but is it always a car? When it is being assembled in the factory, at what point does it stop being a set of parts and become a car? One answer is that it becomes a car when it can fulfill the function of a car—that is, when it can be driven. But does that mean it stops being a car if it won't start? What if the car's wheels were stolen; would it still be a car? What is the essence of this thing we call "car"?

Another aspect of this idea is that things aren't inherently either good or bad. Things may seem good or bad depending on the context, but nothing is good or bad in its essence.

Think of something you usually consider either good or bad. Then try to think of contexts where it might seem different—when something you think of as good seems bad, or vice versa. Write down the thing and the contexts where it seems different.

111

Buddhism

The Farmer's Horse

Buddhism often uses stories to present ideas. Here is a Buddhist story. Read it. Then, in the space below, write what idea you think the story is trying to present.

One day a farmer's only horse disappeared. His neighbors all came to commiserate with him on his bad luck. But the farmer just said, "Bad luck? Good luck? Who knows?"

A week or so later, the farmer's horse returned, accompanied by two wild horses. His neighbors all came by to congratulate him on his good luck. But the farmer just said, "Good luck? Bad luck? Who knows?"

The farmer's son decided to break the wild horses so they could be ridden. One of the horses threw him and broke his leg. The neighbors came by to console the farmer for this stroke of bad luck. But the farmer just said, "Bad luck? Good luck? Who knows?"

A few days later, the king's army came to the village. They took all the able-bodied young men to fight in a war. They left the farmer's son because he had a broken leg. The neighbors all came by to congratulate the farmer on his good luck. But the farmer just said, "Good luck? Bad luck? Who knows?"

112

Buddhism

The Strawberry

Buddhism often uses stories to present ideas. Here is a Buddhist story. Read it. Then, in the space below, write what idea you think the story is trying to present.

One day while walking in the wilderness, a man came upon a vicious tiger. He fled, running through the trees, looking back over his shoulder to see if the tiger was gaining on him. Unfortunately, this meant he didn't watch where he was going, and he tumbled headlong over a cliff. He scrabbled desperately to save himself and managed to grab a vine that hung over the cliff. For a few moments he dangled there, savoring his amazing escape from certain death. Then he looked up. Two mice were perched on the cliff edge, gnawing on his vine with their sharp little teeth.

As he looked up, the man glimpsed something else. A strawberry plant was growing from the cliff face, with one plump, ripe strawberry. The man reached up and plucked the strawberry. It was incredibly delicious!

113

Buddhism

Rainy Day, Sunny Day

Buddhism often uses stories to present ideas. Here is a Buddhist story. Read it. Then, in the space below, write what idea you think the story is trying to present.

An old lady had two daughters. One was married to an umbrella seller. The other was married to a noodle seller. On sunny days, the woman worried about her first daughter, thinking that nobody would buy any umbrellas, and her son-in-law's business would be hurt. On rainy days, she worried about her second daughter, as her son-in-law couldn't dry noodles without the sun. As a result, the old lady lived in sorrow, grieving for her daughters.

One day she met a monk who asked her why she seemed so grief-stricken. She told him about her worries. The monk smiled and said, "I will show you a way to happiness. On sunny days, think of the younger daughter's husband making plenty of noodles and doing good business. On rainy days, think of the older daughter's husband. With the rain, people will be buying umbrellas, and the business will prosper."

The woman did as the monk told her. From then on she was happy every day.

114

Buddhism

The Law of Karma

The law of *karma* is part of Buddhist teaching. The law of karma involves cause and effect. It says that every event causes another event. The second event can be pleasant or unpleasant, depending on whether the first event was prompted by self-interested cravings or by pure motivations. The second event can be so far separated from the first one that they don't seem to be connected, but the connection is still there. If our actions come from pure motivations, then the results will be positive, leading us to keep acting in positive ways. If we are motivated by negative feelings, then the results of our actions will also be negative. And the effects of negative feelings can be cumulative. When bad things happen to us, we tend to respond negatively. This can lead to a vicious circle of negative actions and negative results.

Think of something negative that has happened to you. Then think of how you reacted to it. If you reacted negatively, did that negative reaction also affect the way you saw other things? If you reacted positively, did that positive reaction affect your outlook in positive ways? Write two or three sentences describing the event, your reaction, and how your reaction affected you.

115

Buddhism

Arhat and Bodhisattva

In Buddhism, people can attain enlightenment in many ways. They can also do different things once they are enlightened. One choice is to enter nirvana, where all suffering ends. A person who chooses this is called an *arhat*. A second choice is to stay in the world to help others find enlightenment. A person who chooses this is called a *bodhisattva*.

The difference between them is explained in a story. Two men were wandering in the desert when they came to a compound, surrounded by a high wall. The first man climbed the wall. Giving a cry of delight, he leaped down on the other side. The second man also climbed the wall. At the top, he saw that the walls surrounded a beautiful oasis with springs and gardens. He wanted to enter the garden. But he thought about all the other people who were wandering in the desert. Instead of entering the oasis he returned to the desert, determined to help other wanderers find the oasis.

One of these men was an arhat, and one was a bodhisattva. Which was which?

116

Buddhism

Non-Buddhist Bodhisattvas

A *bodhisattva* is a person who has achieved enlightenment and is dedicated to helping other people escape from suffering. Some teachers suggest that non-Buddhists might be bodhisattvas.

Can you think of anyone (either from history or the present day) who fits the description of a bodhisattva? Name as many people as you can.

117

Buddhism

The Ten Perfections of a Bodhisattva

In Buddhism, a bodhisattva struggles to achieve ten perfections. Only when these have been achieved can the bodhisattva become a buddha. The ten perfections are charity, right conduct, dispassionateness, wisdom, steadfastness, forbearance, truthfulness, determination, loving compassion, and nonattachability.

Think about the ten perfections. How do you think they can be achieved? Choose one perfection. Describe how a person could achieve it.

118

Buddhism

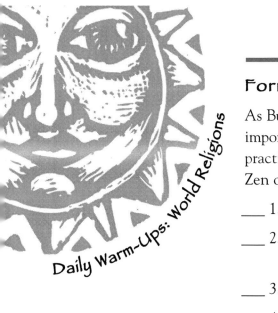

Forms of Buddhism

As Buddhism spread from India, it developed different forms. Two important forms are Zen and Tibetan Buddhism. The ideas and practices listed below belong to one of these two forms. Write **Z** for Zen or **T** for Tibetan beside each one.

___ 1. studying *koans*, or riddlelike problems

___ 2. using *mandalas*, a graphic symbol of the universe, to draw the eye into spiritual pursuits

___ 3. practicing *tonglen*, a meditation of compassion

___ 4. achieving *satori*, a flash of understanding that brings a new perspective on the world

___ 5. studying *Tantras*, texts that deal with the interrelatedness of things

___ 6. performing *zazen*, a sitting meditation

119

Buddhism

Koans

Do you remember learning how to read? Most people are taught the letters of the alphabet and are told that these letters can form sounds. But this is a new way of thinking, and it takes time to adjust to it. For most people, the next step, recognizing words and sounds, is a breakthrough. Suddenly, the marks on the page make sense. They can read.

According to Zen Buddhism, enlightenment also calls for a new way of thinking. We are used to solving problems using reason. But enlightenment isn't reasonable. So Zen uses unreasonable ways of teaching to help students reach enlightenment.

One unreasonable teaching method is the use of *koans*. These are problems, but problems that rational thinking can't solve. In order to find an answer to a koan, the student must think in a different way. One koan asks, "What was the appearance of your face before your ancestors were born?"

How do you think it would feel to be given problems like this one to solve? Try to imagine your reaction to solving koans. Write a description of your reaction here.

Buddhism

Tonglen

Tibetan Buddhists have a visualization practice called *tonglen*. This is a way of awakening the compassion that lies within all people, as well as a way of overcoming the fear of suffering.

Try practicing *tonglen* yourself. Think of a person with a specific problem like sickness, greed, or meanness. Try to pick a person you don't especially like. Close your eyes. Imagine that you are lifting this problem out of his or her body and taking it into your own body, where it is destroyed.

How did your attempt at *tonglen* feel? Do you think that practicing it often would change your attitude to the person you chose? Write two or three sentences in explanation.

Daily Warm-Ups: World Religions

121

Buddhism

Bowing

Another Buddhist practice is bowing to the Buddha. This is not a slight bow from the waist, but a full prostration. The practitioner's knees, forearms, and forehead all touch the ground.

Bowing sounds like an easy way to practice Buddhism. Proper bowing, though, requires physical, mental, and spiritual awareness. It is not enough to bow because other people bow, or because you want other people to think well of you because you are devoted. While you are bowing, your mind can't wander. You can't think about getting something to eat as soon as you're done bowing. You need to focus on bowing, on the Buddha's teachings, and on the Buddha-nature.

122

How do you think that bowing in this way could help a student of Buddhism? Write two or three sentences for your answer.

Buddhism

The Four Immeasurables

Everyone wants to be happy, but according to Buddhism, there is no such thing as individual happiness. Because all people are interconnected, the happiness of one person depends on the happiness of all people. In order to be happy, all people must develop positive attitudes toward all other people and sentient beings. One way to do this is through the Four Immeasurables.

The Four Immeasurables are four positive states of mind. They are called immeasurable both because they are directed toward an immeasurable number of other beings and because the amount of good karma they create is immeasurable. The Four Immeasurables are loving-kindness, compassion, appreciative joy, and equanimity. Loving-kindness is the wish that all sentient beings should be happy—not just the people we like, but all people and animals. Compassion is the wish for all sentient beings to be free from suffering. Appreciative joy involves rejoicing in the happiness of others, not just our own happiness. Equanimity calls for regarding all sentient beings as our equals.

123

How do you think developing the Four Immeasurables can contribute to happiness? Write two or three sentences for your answer.

Buddhism

Bad Habits, Good Habits

The Buddha was a person and not a god. The lesson of his life is that people can live without suffering in a state of happiness. What can a person do to stop his or her suffering? Like the Buddha, each person has to experiment to find a way to enlightenment. The first step is to identify habits that interfere with happiness and habits that can help lead to enlightenment.

List your own bothersome bad habits. Also list some good habits of yours that might lead to profound happiness.

124

Christianity

Facts About Christianity

Here are some facts about Christianity. Use them to write an informational paragraph about this widespread religion in the space below.

- About 2,000 years old
- Based on the life and teachings of Jesus of Nazareth
- Has only one God
- Followers believe that Jesus was the Christ and that he died and was restored to life.
- Followers worship in churches.
- Has two billion followers worldwide
- Has many branches, including Catholicism, Eastern Orthodoxy, and various Protestant denominations, including Baptist, Lutheran, and Anglican
- Religious text is the Bible, which is made up of the Old Testament and New Testament.

125

Christianity

The Life of Jesus

Christianity is based on the teachings of Jesus. His life is sometimes summarized like this: He was born in a stable. He didn't go to college, and he wrote no books. He worked as a carpenter. At the age of thirty-three, he was executed as a criminal.

Does this sound like the life story of someone who ended up changing the world? Write three or four sentences for your answer.

Daily Warm-Ups: World Religions

126

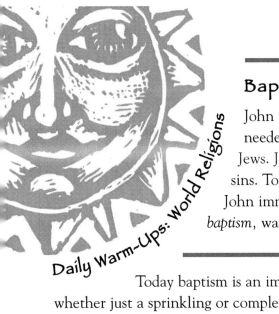

Baptism

John the Baptist was a Jewish prophet. He told people that they
needed to prepare for the coming of the *Messiah,* or deliverer of the
Jews. John urged people to repent and to seek forgiveness for their
sins. To show their repentance, people came to John to be baptized.
John immersed his followers in the Jordan River. This immersion, or
baptism, was symbolic. It signified spiritual cleansing and rebirth.

Today baptism is an important Christian ceremony. The ceremony still involves water,
whether just a sprinkling or complete immersion. Why do you think water is used in
this ceremony? Write two or three sentences for your answer.

Daily Warm-Ups: World Religions

127

Christianity

Jesus Chooses His Apostles

Jesus had many disciples, or followers. He chose some of the disciples to be his close companions. They are known as the apostles. An *apostle* is a person who is sent on a mission. Jesus's apostles went out to spread his message, which became the foundation of Christianity.

This passage from the Bible describes Jesus's selection of the apostles.

> At daybreak he called his disciples and selected twelve of them to be his apostles: Simon, to whom he gave the name Peter, and Andrew his brother, James and John, Philip and Bartholomew, Matthew and Thomas, James son of Alphaeus, and Simon called the Zealot, Judas son of James, and Judas Iscariot, who turned traitor. (Luke 6:13–16)

How many apostles were there? Name them all.

Christianity

Temptation

According to Christianity, temptation is an obstacle we all face in life. Jesus himself had to deal with temptation from a *devil*, a spirit that seeks to convince someone to disobey God's will. The devil asked Jesus to turn a stone into bread and prove his miraculous powers. He offered Jesus all the riches of the world if he would follow him. Jesus said no to these offers.

Do you think temptation is a part of everyone's life? What kinds of temptation do you face? How do you deal with temptation? Write three or four sentences for your answer.

129

Christianity

Jesus and the Money Changers

Passover is a special date in the Jewish calendar. In Jesus's time, people traveled great distances to spend Passover in Jerusalem. Part of the Passover ritual involved sacrificing animals and paying a tax to the temple. Since this tax needed to be paid in local currency, people from other areas had to have their money changed. Those who made long journeys could not bring their own animals for sacrifice, so they bought them in Jerusalem.

Jesus, who was a Jew, went to Jerusalem at Passover time. Here is an account of his visit from the Bible.

As the Jewish Passover was near, Jesus went up to Jerusalem. In the temple precincts he came upon people engaged in selling oxen, sheep and doves, and others seated changing coins. He made a whip of cord and drove sheep and oxen alike out of the temple area, and knocked over the money-changers' tables, spilling their coins. He told those who were selling doves: "Get them out of here! Stop turning my Father's house into a marketplace!" (John 2:13–16)

If worshippers needed to buy animals and change money, why do you think Jesus reacted in this way? Write three or four sentences for your answer.

Christianity

The Teachings of Jesus

What did Jesus, whose teachings are the basis of Christianity, teach people to do? What was his lesson for the world? He told people to be loving and grateful. He told people to forgive others. He told people to serve the needy and the outcast.

Do you think these teachings are good? Do you try to do some or all of these things?

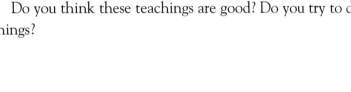

131

Christianity

Pharisees, Sadducees, Essenes, Zealots

When Jesus, whose teachings form the basis of Christianity, was born, Palestine was under Roman rule. Jews were treated badly and had to pay high taxes. Different groups responded to this situation in different ways. One group, the Sadducees, tried to make the best of things. They accepted Roman rule and tried to fit in with Roman society. Another group, the Essenes, thought the situation in Palestine came about because the world was corrupt. They withdrew from the world into their own independent communities and devoted themselves to a life of piety. A third group, the Pharisees, wanted to change society. They remained within society but tried to make Judaism strong again by sticking strictly to the Jewish code of holiness. A fourth group, the Zealots, also wanted change. They tried to use force to overthrow Roman rule.

132

Based on what you know about the teachings of Jesus, which of these four groups do you think he had most in common with? Write three or four sentences for your explanation.

Christianity

Pharisees and Jesus

The Pharisees were an important Jewish group at the time of Jesus.
They wanted to change society by making Judaism strong again. They
focused on *Mosaic* law—the laws that Moses gave the Jews. The
Pharisees categorized certain things as clean or unclean, such as foods
and the way they were prepared. People who didn't follow these
distinctions were also categorized as unclean. This meant that people who
did certain jobs or who couldn't afford to follow all the rules of the Pharisees,
were seen as less worthy.

Jesus didn't agree with this idea. He saw all people as worthwhile. Jesus was
willing to talk with anyone, even those the Pharisees considered unworthy, such as
sinners, prostitutes, lepers, poor people, and the mentally ill.

This attitude toward people caused conflict between the Pharisees and Jesus
and his followers. Why do you think this might have caused conflict? Write
three or four sentences for your answer.

133

Daily Warm-Ups: World Religions

Christianity

The Lost Sheep

One of the ways Jesus taught his disciples was through parables. *Parables* are vivid stories that have a hidden message. Jesus often used parables to respond to criticism.

The Gospel of Luke is in the New Testament of the Bible. It tells of an incident where Jesus was preaching to a group of tax collectors and sinners.

> . . . at which the Pharisees and the scribes murmured, "This man welcomes sinners and eats with them." Then he addressed this parable to them: "Who among you, if he has a hundred sheep and loses one of them, does not leave the ninety-nine in the wasteland and follow the lost one until he finds it? And when he has found it, he lays it on his shoulders, rejoicing. And when he comes home, he calls together his friends and his neighbors, saying to them, 'Rejoice with me, for I have found my sheep which was lost.' I tell you, there will likewise be more joy in heaven over one repentant sinner than over ninety-nine righteous people who have no need to repent." (Luke 15:2–7)

134

In your own words, explain the message of this parable.

Christianity

The Prodigal Son

The parable of the *prodigal,* or wasteful, son is found in the New Testament of the Bible. It tells of a man and his two sons. The younger son asked for his inheritance, moved to another country, and spent all his money. Once all his money was spent, the younger son was close to starvation. Finally he decided to return to his father. He felt that his father owed him nothing, since he treated his father ungratefully. He planned to ask his father for a job as a servant.

As the son approached the farm, his father saw him and ran to greet him. The father had the servants bring fine robes for his son and prepare a feast.

The older son, who had stayed on the farm, was angry about this. He pointed out that he had always obeyed his father and worked hard, but his father had never thrown a party for him. The father replied, "Son, you are always with me, and everything I have is yours. But we had to celebrate and rejoice! This brother of yours was dead, and is alive; he was lost, and is found." (Luke 15:31–32)

What do you think is the message of this parable? Write three or four sentences for your answer.

135

Christianity

The Rich Fool

In Jesus' time, people who had disputes with others often asked a *rabbi*, or Jewish spiritual leader, to solve the dispute. Because Jesus was seen as a wise teacher, people sometimes asked him to settle their disagreements. One day, a man asked Jesus to settle a dispute about money. Jesus refused, saying, "Who made me a judge or divider over you?" (Luke 12:14) Then he told them this parable, which is found in the Bible.

The land of a rich man brought forth plentifully; and he thought to himself, "What shall I do, for I have nowhere to store my crops?" And he said, "I will do this: I will pull down my barns, and build larger ones; and there I will store all my grain and my goods. And I will say to my soul, Soul, you have ample goods laid up for many years; take your ease, eat, drink, be merry." But God said to him, "Fool! This night your soul is required of you; and the things you have prepared, whose will they be?" So is he who lays up treasure for himself, and is not rich toward God. (Luke 12:16–21)

136

What do you think is the meaning of this parable? Write two or three sentences for your answer.

Christianity

The Golden Rule

In his sermons, Jesus gave his listeners advice on how to live, such as this:

> Treat others the way you would have them treat you: this sums up the law and the prophets. (Matthew 7:12)

Do you think this is a good approach to dealing with people? Do you treat people in this way? Write two or three sentences for your answer.

137

© 2004 Walch Publishing

Christianity

Love of Enemies

Jesus urged his followers to love other people, even those who hurt them. He said:

> My command to you is: love your enemies, pray for your persecutors. This will prove that you are sons of your heavenly Father, for his sun rises on the bad and the good, he rains on the just and the unjust. If you love those who love you, what merit is there in that? Do not tax collectors do as much? And if you greet your brothers only, what is so praiseworthy about that? Do not pagans do as much? (Matthew 5: 44–47)

What reasons does Jesus give here for trying to love everyone, not just friends and family? Write two or three sentences for your answer.

138

Christianity

The Treasure and the Pearl

In one of his parables found in the Bible, Jesus described the kingdom of heaven.

> The kingdom of heaven is like treasure hidden in a field, which a man found and covered up; then in his joy he goes and sells all that he has and buys that field. Again, the kingdom of heaven is like a merchant in search of fine pearls, who, on finding one pearl of great value, went and sold all that he had and bought it. (Matthew 13:44–46)

What do you think is the message of this parable? Write three or four sentences to explain it.

139

Christianity

The Good Samaritan

Jesus told this parable of the Good Samaritan in response to the question, "What must I do to inherit everlasting life?" (Luke 10:25)

A man was going down from Jerusalem to Jericho, and he fell among robbers, who stripped him and beat him, and departed, leaving him half dead. Now by chance a priest was going down that road; and when he saw him he passed by on the other side. So likewise a Levite[1], when he came to the place and saw him, passed by on the other side. But a Samaritan[2], as he journeyed, came to where he was; and when he saw him, he had compassion, and went to him and bound up his wounds, pouring on oil and wine; then he set him on his own beast and brought him to an inn, and took care of him. And the next day he took out two denarii[3] and gave them to the innkeeper, saying, "Take care of him; and whatever more you spend, I will repay you when I come back." Which of these three, do you think, proved neighbor to the man who fell among the robbers? He said, "The one who showed mercy on him." And Jesus said to him, "Go and do likewise." (Luke 10:30–37)

[1]Levites were Jews who performed duties in the Temple.
[2]Samaritans were people from Samaria; most Jews looked down on them.
[3]a unit of money

In your own words, explain the message of this parable.

Christianity

Paralyzed

According to the Gospel of Mark in the Bible, Jesus was in Capernaum when a group of men brought a paralyzed friend to see him. Most of the people around Jesus assumed that the paralyzed person was guilty of some sin, and they were afraid of sin. Jesus told the man that he was forgiven. Then he told him to get up and walk.

When someone has a difficulty that we do not share, we may assume that they did something bad to make it happen. Is this fair? Write two or three sentences for your answer.

141

Christianity

Blindness

In the town of Jericho, Jesus helped a blind man named Bartimaeus regain his sight. Without touching the man's eyes or making a big show of it, Jesus said, "Go your way, your faith has made you well."

You know what it means to be literally blind. What does it mean to be figuratively blind? Write two or three sentences for your answer.

142

Christianity

The Imagery of Jesus

In his teaching, Jesus used everyday language. His lessons were based on things his listeners were familiar with. He spoke of shepherds and sheep, of rocky soil and mustard seed. These were all part of daily life in Palestine at that time.

Do you think Jesus' message would have affected people as much if he had spoken in terms of heaven and angels, not rocks and farmers? Explain your answer.

143

The Wild Man of Gerasenes

According to the Gospel of Mark in the Bible, a man near Gerasenes was possessed by an army of demons. The man was a source of fear for the local people. He had been living in a tomb, hitting himself with rocks, and yelling wildly at night. Jesus helped the man transfer his demons onto a flock of pigs, and the pigs ran over a cliff.

Daily Warm-Ups: World Religions

Would you have been able to approach a wild man like the one in Gerasenes? What would have kept you away from him? Why do you think Jesus approached him? Write three or four sentences for your answer.

144

Christianity

The Conversion of Saul

According to the Acts of the Apostles in the Bible, a man named Saul was a *Pharisee*, or conservative Jew. He was active in the fight to stop Jesus from preaching. One day Saul was going to Damascus to arrest any followers of Jesus he might find. As he rode along, a light flashed in front of him, and he fell to the ground, blinded.

. . . and at the same time heard a voice saying, "Saul, Saul, why do you persecute me?" "Who are you, sir?" he asked. The voice answered, "I am Jesus, the one you are persecuting. Get up and go into the city, where you will be told what to do." (Acts 9:4–6)

For several days, Saul could not see. He converted to Christianity and took the name Paul. His sight returned when he was baptized. Now instead of persecuting Christians, Paul became an active preacher in Jesus's name.

145

Saul had a dramatic moment of spiritual awakening. However, spiritual awakening does not need to be so dramatic. Have you ever had a moment when you felt spiritually aware? Write three or four sentences describing the experience.

Christianity

Grace

According to Christianity, to have "grace" is to experience the unconditional love and the forgiveness of God.

What does it mean to experience unconditional love? How would a person know he or she was experiencing grace? Write two or three sentences for your answer.

146

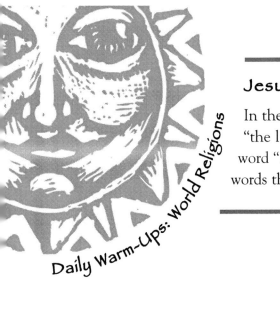

Daily Warm-Ups: World Religions

Christianity

Jesus as Light

In the New Testament of the Bible, Jesus and God are often called "the light." Why is that? What associations do you have with the word "light"? From what you know of Christianity, are there other words that could describe Jesus or God symbolically? Write them here.

147

Christianity

The Miracle of the Loaves and Fishes

Jesus was teaching a crowd of 5,000 people on a hill beside the sea of Galilee. The people became hungry. A boy brought Jesus an offering of five barley loaves and two fish. According to the Gospel of John in the Bible, Jesus blessed the offering and distributed the bread and fish throughout the crowd until no one was hungry.

Daily Warm-Ups: World Religions

Everyone knows that it is important to eat literally, but what is the figurative meaning of this story? What does Jesus do for his listener? Write three or four sentences for your answer.

148

Christianity

The Parable of the Sower

Several of Jesus' apostles recorded this parable.

> A sower went out to sow his seed; and as he sowed, some fell along the path, and was trodden under foot, and the birds of the air devoured it. And some fell on the rock; and as it grew up, it withered away, because it had no moisture. And some fell among thorns; and the thorns grew with it and choked it. And some fell into good soil and grew, and yielded a hundredfold.
>
> (Luke 8:4–15)

Jesus then explained that the seed in the parable was the word of God. In that case, what is the meaning of the parable? Explain it in your own words.

149

Christianity

Have no Fear

Jesus took the apostles Peter, James, and John to the top of a mountain. His friends saw an aura around Jesus. Then the Jewish prophets Moses and Elijah appeared. Jesus' face was like a sun. His clothes became white as light. According to the Gospel of Matthew in the Bible, Jesus said to his disciples "rise and have no fear."

What does it mean to have no fear? How would your life be different if you didn't have any fear? Write two or three sentences for your answer.

150

Christianity

The Last Supper

At the Last Supper, Jesus met with his disciples for the last time before his death. He knew that he would be betrayed by Judas Iscariot and denied by Peter, two good friends. Nevertheless, he promised them his eternal love. Jesus said that a Holy Spirit would guide his followers.

All people need guidance. Where do you get your guidance from? How do you decide when to take guidance from a particular person? Write two or three sentences for your answer.

151

Christianity

The Importance of Love

Soon after Jesus' death, his followers started to teach about his life and deeds. One such man was Paul. Paul was a Jew who had a spiritual conversion on the road to Damascus and spent the rest of his life traveling and teaching about Jesus. Paul believed that all people sin and all people can receive the grace of God. According to I Corinthians, one of the books of the New Testament, Paul said that love is the greatest thing.

How might love be the "greatest thing"? Write two or three sentences for your answer.

152

Christianity

Doing Good Works

Not long after Jesus' death, the apostle Peter was speaking to a group who knew nothing about Jesus. He needed to summarize what Jesus had done. Part of his summary was simple: "He went about doing good works."

How do you imagine Peter's audience might have responded to this description of Jesus? Write three or four sentences for your answer.

153

Islam

Facts About Islam

Here are some facts about Islam. Use them to write an informational paragraph about this widespread religion in the space below.

- Has about 1.3 billion followers worldwide

- Founded in about 610 C.E. by the prophet Muhammad

- Five Pillars of Islam: declaration of faith, prayer, charity, fasting, pilgrimage to Mecca

- Monotheistic (a belief in one God, Allah)

    - Holy city is Mecca, Saudia Arabia

    - Holy book is the Qur'an (Koran)

    - Followers worship in mosques; their spritual leaders are called imams.

154

Daily Warm-Ups: World Religions

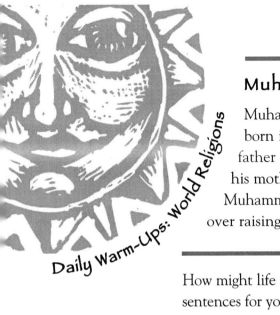

Islam

Muhammad

Muhammad, the founder and most important prophet of Islam, was born in 570 C.E. in the town of Mecca on the Arabian Peninsula. His father died a few days before Muhammad was born. When he was six, his mother died, and he was given into his grandfather's care. When Muhammad was eight, his grandfather also died. His uncle then took over raising Muhammad.

How might life experiences like these affect someone? Write three or four sentences for your answer.

155

Islam

The Meaning of Muhammad

Stories say that when Muhammad's mother was pregnant, a voice said to her, "You are pregnant with the lord of this people. When he is born, say, 'I put him in the care of the One from the evil of every envier'; then call him Muhammad."

The name *Muhammad* means "highly praised." Muhammad did, indeed, grow up to be highly praised. When his name is spoken or written, it is customary for Muslims, followers of Islam, to utter the blessing "peace be upon him."

Today, more boys in the world are given the name "Muhammad" than any other name.

156

Why do you think the name "Muhammad" is so popular today? Write two or three sentences for your answer.

Daily Warm-Ups: World Religions

Islam

Muhammad's Roles in Life

Muhammad, Islam's founder, had many roles in life: husband, father, shepherd, merchant, hermit, exile, leader, prophet, soldier.

Think about the kinds of personal traits a person would need to succeed in all these different roles. List as many of them as you can.

Islam

Society in Muhammad's Time

The world into which Muhammad, the founder of Islam, was born was chaotic. The Arabian Peninsula was an important trading center. The cities of Arabia acted independently. Different cities often raided trading caravans bringing goods to another city. Even within one city, different tribes carried on blood feuds. To rise in society, a man needed the protection of a powerful tribe. Women had no rights; they were little more than possessions of their fathers and husbands.

Muhammad was a deeply moral man, who thought a great deal about ethical issues. How do you think an ethical person might have looked at the society of the day? Write three or four sentences for your answer.

158

Muhammad as Shepherd

The life of a shepherd is often quiet and lonely. A shepherd could spend days alone with his thoughts, not seeing or talking to any other people.

As a boy and young man, Muhammad worked as a shepherd. He watched flocks of sheep in the hills outside Mecca, protecting them from attackers, both human and animal.

Later Muhammad became a successful merchant. But he was also a deeply moral man who thought about the ills of society. In his forties, Muhammad began to spend time alone in a cave in the mountains thinking. On one of his visits to the cave he had a vision. An angel appeared and told Muhammad that he was the appointed prophet of *Allah,* or God.

How do you think Muhammad's early days as a shepherd contributed to his ability to spend time alone thinking? Write three or four sentences for your answer.

159

Daily Warm-Ups: World Religions

Islam

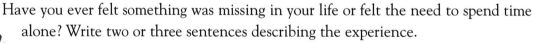

Muhammad as Seeker

When Islam's founder, Muhammad, was a young man, he became a merchant. He worked for a wealthy businesswoman named Khadijah. Khadijah was impressed with Muhammad's honesty, generosity, and gentleness. She and Muhammad were married.

Muhammad and Khadijah had four daughters and two sons. After fifteen years of marriage, Muhammad became aware that something was missing in his life, and he began to retreat to a mountain cave.

Have you ever felt something was missing in your life or felt the need to spend time alone? Write two or three sentences describing the experience.

160

Islam

A New Idea

Muhammad believed that there was only one God, Allah. When he began preaching the message of Allah, he met with opposition. The society in which Muhammad lived was *polytheistic*—that is, it believed in many gods. Mecca, where he lived, was a religious center. There were 360 shrines to different gods in Mecca; the city received considerable income from pilgrims to these shrines.

Think of some other time when a new idea was not accepted at first. It could be an event in your own life or something from history or current events. Write about it in two to three sentences.

161

Islam

The Hegira

Muhammad, Islam's most important prophet, became an outcast in his home city, because people in Mecca disapproved of Muhammad's messages and religion. People in another city, Yathrib, asked Muhammad to leave Mecca and become their leader.

Knowing the opposition he faced in Mecca, Muhammad accepted their invitation. Threatened with violence in Mecca, Muhammad and his followers made their way secretly to Yathrib. This emigration is known as the *Hegira*. The Islamic calendar begins with the Hegira, which was July 16, 622, in the Western calendar.

In Yathrib, Muhammad became a successful politician. Yathrib became known as Medinat al-Nabi, or City of the Prophet, then simply Medina.

Within ten years of his flight to Medina, Mecca surrendered to Muhammad. By the time he died, in June 632 C.E., Muhammad had united the disparate peoples of the Arabian Peninsula into one nation.

162

Write two or three sentences describing what it must be like to be forced to flee your home, like Muhammad.

Islam

Muhammad as Political Leader

After years of being harassed, Muhammad and his followers went to a town called Yathrib. According to Islam, two tribes from Yathrib, the Auws and Khazraj, approached Muhammad and invited him to govern their town which was prone to civil war. Muhammad needed a place where his followers could live in peace, without fear of persecution, so he agreed. The city was soon called Medina. Muhammad wrote a charter for its citizens and established a peace.

What does this tell us about Muhammad? Write two or three sentences for your answer.

163

Daily Warm-Ups: World Religions

Islam

The Ascension of Muhammad

After eleven years outside Mecca, Muhammad, Islam's founder, experienced an Ascension, in which he journeyed to heaven. After praying, Muhammad was approached by the angel Gabriel. They mounted a winged steed called the *buraq* and traveled to Jerusalem, where the spirits of many prophets appeared. Muhammad led them in prayer. Then he remounted the *buraq* and ascended with Gabriel to heaven.

Muhammad said that heaven was difficult to describe. He said it was a combination of lights and sounds and flowing energy.

164

What does the word *heaven* mean to you? What do you imagine heaven looks like? Write three or four sentences for your answer.

Allah Prescribes Prayer

During Muhammad's Night Journey to heaven, he was led into the presence of Allah. Allah said that Muslims were to pray fifty times each day. On Muhammad's way back to Earth, he met with Moses, who asked, "What has Allah told your followers to do?" Muhammad answered that Allah wanted the faithful to pray fifty times a day. Moses urged Muhammad to return to Allah and ask Him to reduce the number of prayers, as Muhammad's followers would not be able to pray that many times. So Muhammad went back to Allah, and Allah reduced the number of prayers to forty each day. Moses insisted that this was still too much, and sent Muhammad back to Allah. This happened several times; each time, Allah reduced the number of prayers, until the requirement stood at five prayers a day. Moses insisted that this was still too much, as he had tried to get people to pray in the past, and they could not accomplish this. Muhammad replied, "I have already returned to my Lord till I am ashamed. I am satisfied, and I submit."

What do these events tell you about the prophets and their followers?

165

Islam

Surrender

The word *Islam* means "surrender to the will of God." The word *Muslim* means "one who has surrendered."

How do you think a deep sense of religious conviction can be seen as surrender? Write two or three sentences for your answer.

Daily Warm-Ups: World Religions

The Qur'an

The Islamic holy book is known as the Qur'an, or Koran. The word *Qur'an* means "recitation." It records Muhammad's revelations from Allah.

Until about 650 C.E., the Qur'an existed only in oral form. Muhammad shared his revelations with his followers, who memorized his words. Then about twenty years after Muhammad's death, all the revelations were gathered together in written form.

Some Muslims objected to writing down Muhammad's revelations. They said that if Muhammad had wanted these revelations committed to writing, he would have asked his followers to do this during his lifetime. Other leaders felt that it was essential. Their view prevailed, and the written Qur'an was prepared.

What reasons can you think of for writing down the revelations of Muhammad? List as many reasons as you can.

167

© 2004 Walch Publishing

Islam

Prohibited Acts

Devout Muslims dedicate themselves to cultivating certain virtues and avoiding vices. Muslims are prohibited from doing many things. They include spiritual prohibitions: Muslims should not deny the revelation of God to his prophets, swear falsely in the name of God, or lose hope in the mercy of God. They also include behavioral prohibitions: Muslims should not deliberately kill another human being, lie, steal, cheat, betray their country, commit adultery, gamble, drink alcohol, oppress the people or aid an oppressor, or deliberately hinder a good cause.

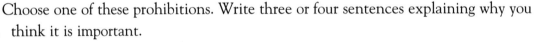

Choose one of these prohibitions. Write three or four sentences explaining why you think it is important.

168

Islam

The Gift of Life

In Islam, life is considered a gift from Allah. Accepting this gift leaves us with two obligations. First, we must show our gratitude for this gift. Second, in return for this gift, we must give ourselves to Allah by surrendering ourselves to his wishes.

Do you believe that life is a "gift?" Explain why or why not. Write two or three sentences for your answer.

169

Islam

Time Line of Islam

Here are some important events in the early history of Islam. Use your knowledge of Islam and of the history of the region to determine their correct order. Number the events from 1 to 10, with 1 as the earliest event.

___ a. Uthman dies; Ali, Muhammad's son-in-law, becomes the fourth caliph.

___ b. Muhammad dies; Abu Bakr becomes the first caliph, or successor to Muhammad.

___ c. Muhammad marries Khadijah.

___ d. Umar dies; Uthman becomes the third caliph.

___ e. Muhammad migrates to Medina; the Islamic calendar begins.

___ f. Muhammad is born.

___ g. Islam spreads to Samarkand in the North, India in the East, and North Africa and Spain in the West.

___ h. Abu Bakr dies; Umar becomes the second caliph; Islam spreads to Egypt, Syria, Iran.

___ i. Muslims conquer Mecca.

___ j. Muhammad receives the first revelation from Allah.

170

Islam

The Five Pillars of Islam

Islam includes five major principles known as the Five Pillars of Islam. These pillars are *Shahadah*, declaring one's faith in Allah; *salat*, daily prayer; *zakat*, giving to charity; *saum*, fasting during the holy month of Ramadan; and *hajj*, making a pilgrimage to the holy city of Mecca.

Many different cultures and religions have pillars or underlying principles that set them apart. Think of a group, religion, or other organization that has specific pillars. Write two or three sentences explaining these pillars and showing how they make the group unique.

171

Islam

The First Pillar of Islam: The Profession of Faith

The first Pillar of Islam, the *Shahadah*, is to say, "There is no god except Allah, and I declare that Muhammad is the Messenger of Allah." This declaration of faith asserts that Allah is all, and Allah alone is worthy of our total attention.

What are the benefits of declaring a belief aloud? Write two or three sentences for your answer.

Daily Warm-Ups: World Religions

172

Islam

The Second Pillar of Islam: Prayer

The second Pillar of Islam, *salat,* is the ritual of praying five times a day. There are two focuses one can have in prayer. The first, *salat,* consists of praising Allah. The second, known as *du'a,* or "calling on Allah," means asking Allah for something.

What is the difference between praising Allah and asking Allah for help? Write three or four sentences for your answer.

173

Islam

The Third Pillar of Islam: Charity

The third Pillar of Islam is called *zakat*. It means charity or dues to the poor. There are certain requirements to be met before one can give the *zakat*. One must be an adult, have savings, and have paid all of one's regular expenses. If these things are in order, Muslims pay 2.5% of their wealth to charity or government programs. The purpose of this Pillar is to remind Muslims that those who are in need are entitled to assistance. The *zakat* purifies people of attachment to wealth and reminds them of Allah's generosity.

174

The material world is said to distract people from leading a good life. Does a desire for money keep people from making the right decisions in life? Write two or three sentences to explain your opinion.

Islam

The Fourth Pillar of Islam: Fasting

The fourth Pillar of Islam is *saum*, or fasting. In the ninth month of the lunar calender of Islam, the faithful fast from dawn to dusk. During the fast, Muslims must abstain from eating, drinking, lying, and sensual contact. The fast is meant to help Muslims overcome personal gluttony and the habit of always desiring more.

According to Islam, people struggle to master their bodies and emotions. Fasting helps them with this.

When you want something, is it hard to deny it to yourself? Do you think that practice at denying ourselves things we want would be good for us? Write three or four sentences for your answer.

175

Islam

The Fifth Pillar of Islam: The Hajj

The fifth Pillar of Islam is the *hajj*, or pilgrimage. This consists of a journey to Mecca in Saudi Arabia and circling the Ka'bah, a small building made of bricks and covered with a heavy black cloth. The Ka'bah is believed to be the center of monotheism. Abraham himself built the shrine in the Ka'bah, and Muhammad restored it to a place for worshiping Allah alone (not idols).

During the pilgrimage, Muslims recall the success of Hagar and Ishmael, the prophet Abraham's concubine and their son. Hagar and Ishmael were aided by Allah after they were abandoned by Abraham in the Arabian desert. Pilgrims visit the barren Plain of Arafah to be reminded of the Day of Judgment and throw rocks at stone pillars representing *Shaytan*, the spirit of evil. They also pray regularly. Every year, millions of Muslims perform the hajj.

Most of us have had some experience of being part of a large group of people focused on the same thing, such as at a sporting event or a concert. Think about an experience like this that you have had. Did the energy of the group affect you in any way? Write three or four sentences describing the experience.

176

Daily Warm-Ups: World Religions

© 2004 Walch Publishing

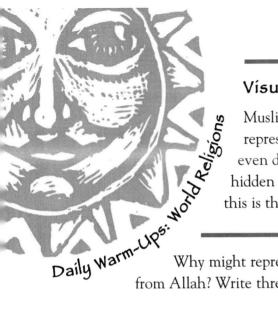

Islam

Visual Representations

Muslims do not believe that Allah or the prophets should be visually represented. According to Islam, representations are misleading and even disrespectful. If Muhammad is shown in a painting, his face is hidden by a veil. Usually a flame is shown burning around his head; this is the flame of prophethood.

Why might representations of Allah and the prophets actually lead people away from Allah? Write three or four sentences for your answer.

177

© 2004 Walch Publishing

Islam

The Noble Writers

According to the Qur'an, we are followed throughout our lives by *Kiraman Katibeen*, the Noble Writers. These two angels sit on our shoulders and record our good and bad actions in a book of deeds.

If you knew that everything you did would be recorded, would you act differently? In what way? Write three or four sentences for your answer.

178

Sufi Stories: The Drum

Sufis are Muslim mystics. They help people to escape worldly interests by becoming aware of spiritual things. Sufis often use stories as part of their teaching. Read the following Sufi story. Then answer the questions that follow.

There was once a small boy who banged a drum all day long. His parents and neighbors were at their wits' ends; no matter what they said, the boy would not be quiet.

Various experts came to help. The first told the boy that he would perforate his eardrums. The second told the boy that beating a drum was a sacred activity and should only be done on special occasions. Other experts offered the neighbors earplugs, gave the boy a book to distract him, gave the neighbors books on how to control their anger, and gave the boy meditation exercises to calm him. The boy kept beating his drum.

Finally a Sufi came along. He looked at the boy and the drum, then pointed to a hammer and chisel lying nearby and said, "I wonder what is *inside* the drum?"

179

Why do the solutions of the "experts" fail? What do you think happens after the Sufi makes his comment?

Islam

Sufi Stories: The Ring

Sufis are Muslim mystics. They help people to escape worldly interests by becoming aware of spiritual things. Sufis often use stories as part of their teaching. Read the following Sufi story. Then explain its message in your own words in the space below.

A powerful king presented a challenge to the wise men of his kingdom.

He said, "I had a dream in which I possessed a ring. The ring helped me bring peace to my state. If I looked upon it when I was unhappy, it made me joyful. If I looked upon it when I was happy, I became sad. Can you find me such a ring?"

The wise men consulted with one another. Finally they found a solution. They had a jeweller make a ring, which they presented to the king. On the ring were engraved the words, "This too will pass."

180

Daily Warm-Ups: World Religions

Answers will vary on pages not listed.

1. Answers will vary.
2. 1. Christianity (2 billion), 2. Islam (1.3 billion), 3. Hinduism (900 million), 4. Buddhism (360 million), 5. Chinese traditional religion (225 million), 6. Sikhism (23 million), 7. Judaism (15 million), 8. Spiritism (14 million), 9. Baha'i (6 million), 10. Jainism (4 million)

3–5. Answers will vary.

6. Answers will vary. Sample answer: Christianity, Islam, and Taoism are all based on the teachings of a single charismatic teacher. Judaism, Islam, and Christianity all have prophets. Judaism, Islam, Christianity, and Taoism all have one primary holy book. Most of these other religions were fundamentally formed at a certain period, and the tenets of the faiths have not changed greatly since they were formed.

7. Paragraphs will vary, but they should be consistent with facts given.

8. Answers will vary. Sample answer: Nepal's isolated location, between India and the Himalayas, makes it less open to influences from countries other than India.

9. Answers will vary.

10. 1. b, 2. e, 3. d, 4. a, 5. f, 6. c

11–16. Answers will vary.

17. Answers will vary. Sample answer: All religions are revelations of God. The revelations appear different because they are developed in different cultures, but they all lead to the same goal: approaching God.

18–19. Answers will vary.

20. Answers will vary. Sample answer: This pose shows that Shiva has triumphed over illusion and ignorance.

21. Answers will vary. Sample answer:

Vishnu moves through progressively higher life forms, just as the soul, or atman, progresses through life forms in the process of samsara, or the cycle of reincarnation.

22. Answers will vary. Sample answers: **Pleasure:** Pleasure is too trivial to satisfy human nature. Pleasure is essentially private, and human nature requires something broader for full satisfaction. Also, pleasure is ephemeral; it does not last. For real happiness, people need something permanent. **Worldly success:** Worldly success cannot satisfy human nature because the elements that make up success—wealth, fame, power—are finite. We cannot all be famous; it is a contradiction in terms. We cannot all be powerful; if some have power, some must be powerless. Since these things can only be possessed by some people at a time, not all people, people are in competition for them, and thus their possession is precarious; those who hold power today can easily lose it tomorrow when someone more powerful comes along. Like pleasure, success is ephemeral.

23. Answers will vary.
24. Answers will vary. Students will probably find that being still for one minute is a lot harder than it sounds.
25. Answers will vary.
26. Answers will vary. Sample answer: A guru is someone who helps a student dispel the darkness of ignorance.
27. Answers will vary. Sample answer: India's geographic location means it does not get steady, year-round rain, but monsoon rains—heavy seasonal rains that depend on a seasonal shift of winds. If the rains

do not come, or come too late, then crops in India fail, as they depend on the rains to grow.

28. Answers will vary. Sample answer: All three considered their duty more important than their personal comfort or desires. Rama obeyed his father's command without complaint; Sita insisted on accompanying Rama into exile, even though she did not have to go; and Bharata refused to accept the kingdom, since he believed his brother was the rightful king.

29. Answers will vary. Sample answer: Gandhi epitomized the path of karma yoga, doing one's duty without self-interest in the consequences of one's actions, and also without concern for negative personal consequences. Gandhi was often jailed and ill-treated for his

actions, but he persevered in what he saw as his duty.

30. Answers will vary. Sample answer: The text is describing the atman, or soul, which is constantly reborn in new bodies. Because the atman is eternal, the body that carries it may die, but the atman itself does not die.

31. Answers will vary. In the Upanishads, the owner of the chariot represents the soul.

32. Answers will vary. Sample answer: The story is teaching about the importance of acting in the right way in all situations, even when the right way is not in our own self-interest.

33. Answers will vary. Sample answer: The story means that it is possible to practice nonviolence without letting people take advantage of you. The snake could no

longer use his fangs, but even his hiss
would keep people from mistreating
him. He had carried the sage's teachings
too far.

34–35. Answers will vary.

36. Paragraphs will vary, but they should be
consistent with facts given.

37. 1. c, 2. a, 3. b, 4. e, 5. d

38. Answers will vary. Sample answer: Ruth
Bader Ginsburgh, Adam Sandler, Ethan
Hawke, Sarah Michelle Gellar, Naomi
Watts

39. Answers will vary. Sample answer:
The Jewish monotheistic outlook was
fundamentally different from the
outlook of other peoples in the region,
making it difficult for them to be
assimilated by other nations, even when
their land was conquered.

40. 1. c, 2. g, 3. e, 4. b, 5. j, 6. h, 7. i, 8. a,
9. f, 10. d

41. 1. c, 2. e, 3. h, 4. a, 5. g, 6. b, 7. d, 8. f

42. 1. c, 2. e, 3. b, 4. h, 5. f, 6. g, 7. d, 8. a

43. a. 1949, b. 1933, c. 1916,
d. 1950s–2000s, e. 1948, f. 1939–1945,
g. 1920s–1930s

44–49. Answers will vary.

50. Answers will vary. Sample answer:
Celebrating Passover is a reminder to
the Jews that they owe their freedom to
God, and that freedom carries both joys
and responsibilities.

51. Answers will vary. Sample answer: Yes,
because they include rules to protect
individuals' lives, property, and good
name.

52. There are laws for commandments 6, 8,
9, and 10.

53. Answers will vary.

54. 1. Nevi'im, 2. Torah, 3. Ketuvim,
    4. Ketuvim
55. Answers will vary.
56. Answers will vary. Sample answer: Isaiah is saying that God chose the Israelites, as the "friend" in the story chose land for his vineyard. Like the vineyard owner, God tended to his people, giving them every care. Instead of rewarding Him with the sweet fruit of faith, they turned from him. For this, they would be punished. God would take away his protection from the Israelites.
57. Answers will vary.
58. Hanukkah or Chanukah
59. Answers will vary.
60. Answers will vary. Sample answer: Because a small group of Jews held out for so long against a much larger Roman army, then chose the freedom of death rather than risk slavery through surrender.
61–64. Answers will vary.
65. Answers will vary. Sample answer: Lao Tzu was like nothing Confucius knew anything about. With nothing to compare Lao Tzu to, Confucius could not analyze him.
66–68. Answers will vary.
69. Answers will vary. Sample answer: It means that you can tackle a huge task if you break it down into small parts.
70. Answers will vary. Sample answer: If you can follow a path, it is not the true path of the Tao because the true Tao cannot be seen or touched. If you can say a name aloud, it is not the name of the true path, because the true Tao cannot be expressed in words.
71. Answers will vary. Sample answer: The

cycles of the seasons or of day and night are eternal. The seasons go from spring to summer to autumn to winter; the sun rises and sets every day, but the cycle has no beginning and no end.

72. Answers will vary. Sample answer: building dams to harness the energy of rivers instead of letting rivers flow unimpeded from source to sea; genetically modifying foods to be resistant to insects and diseases

73. Answers will vary. Sample answer: The rapids and waterfall are like life. If we allow ourselves to be carried along by life, and allow it to shape us, we will not be harmed. But if we fight against the natural course of things, our dreams will be dashed against the rocks.

74. Answers will vary. Sample answer: Water is soft and smooth to the touch. If we put our hands in a pool, the water offers no resistance to our touch. And yet simply by flowing steadily in the same path, day after day, year after year, water can carve channels in the hardest rock.

75. Answers will vary. Sample answer: In this story, inaction was the best action the old warrior could take. Since the young warrior's technique was to let his opponent make the first move so that he could spot a weakness, making no move defeated this technique. The old warrior chose inaction as his first move. He then had to maintain his inaction even when he was insulted and spat upon. This can't have been easy; it would have been easier to have reacted to the insults. But by remaining still, despite the insults, he defeated the young warrior.

76–78. Answers will vary.

79. Answers will vary. Sample answer: It means that we can never be absolutely sure of anything; we can't even be sure of who we ourselves are.

80. Answers will vary.

81. Answers will vary. Sample answer: He is saying that some things in life—such as jobs at court—may look very attractive at first, but they can have negative consequences later, when it's too late to back out.

82. Answers will vary. Sample answer: Because a fundamental principle of Taoism is living in accordance with the patterns of nature and the universe, it would make sense to try to understand what those patterns are and how they come to be.

83–89. Answers will vary.

90. Answers will vary. Sample answer: Seeing these things made Siddhartha realize that there could be no happiness in the physical world because humans must suffer, grow old, and die.

91. Answers will vary.

92. Answers will vary. Sample answer: The Buddha's enlightenment meant becoming aware of existence. As a prince, he was unaware of sickness, old age, and death. His path to enlightenment involved progressively becoming aware of more things. Finally he became aware of all things; in his own words, he was—finally—awake.

93. 1. c, 2. a, 3. e, 4. b, 5. d

94. Answers will vary. Sample answer: He meant that people should make up their own minds about things and not accept or believe something because someone else says so, because it agrees with what

you've heard before, or because it satisfies your own opinions.

95–111. Answers will vary.

112. Answers will vary. Sample answer: Nothing is inherently good or bad; it all depends on the circumstances. What looks good may later turn out to be bad, or vice versa.

113. Answers will vary. Sample answer: This story is about the importance of living in the moment. The future is an illusion; all we have is this moment, this now. The strawberry tasted delicious to the man because he didn't think he would ever taste anything again. If we were able to live our lives as if every moment were the only moment, then everything would be as immeasurably wonderful as the taste of that strawberry.

114. Answers will vary. Sample answer: It is saying that we are in control of how we feel; it depends on how we choose to look at things. As long as the old lady thought about the daughter whose business would suffer from that day's weather, she was unhappy, but when she shifted her thinking to look at the positive side of things, she was happy.

115. Answers will vary.

116. The first man was an arhat; he reached nirvana and gladly accepted it. The second man was a bodhisattva; although he could have entered nirvana and left all suffering behind, he stayed in the world of suffering to help others reach nirvana.

117. Answers will vary. Sample answer: Mohandas Gandhi, Martin Luther King Jr., Mother Teresa

118. Answers will vary.

119. 1. Z, 2. T, 3. T, 4. Z, 5. T, 6. Z
120–126. Answers will vary.
127. Answers will vary. Sample answer: As a bath washes off physical dirt, baptism washes away spiritual wrongs. The water used in the ceremony symbolizes this purification.
128. 12; Peter, Andrew, James, John, Philip, Bartholomew, Matthew, Thomas, James, Simon, Judas, Judas Iscariot.
129. Answers will vary.
130. Answers will vary. Sample answer: Although the worshippers needed to do these things, they didn't need to do them right in the temple. The temple should be a place of worship, not a marketplace.
131. Answers will vary.
132. Answers will vary. Sample answer: He had most in common with the Pharisees.

The Sadducees accepted Roman rule and tried to fit in, but Jesus didn't; when he disagreed with something, he spoke up. The Essenes withdrew from the world, instead of trying to change it; Jesus could have withdrawn, but he didn't; he tried to change society. The Zealots used force to try to effect change; Jesus spoke against the use of force and violence. Like the Pharisees, Jesus tried to effect change from within society.
133–135. Answers will vary.
136. Answers will vary. Sample answer: The parable says that possessions and money aren't the most important things in life. People who focus on money and possessions end up losing everything, because they can't take money with them when they die. It's more important

to focus on God in life, because that is a treasure that will last.

137. Answers will vary.
138. God loves bad people and good people, the just and unjust; they're a part of his creation. To be a part of God's community, you must love your enemies as God would.
139. Answers will vary. Sample answer: The man in the parable sold everything he had to buy a field with a treasure. He didn't need to have enough money to buy the treasure, just the field in which it lay. According to Jesus, the kingdom of heaven is also well within our means to afford, but we need to be willing to give up everything else in exchange for it.
140. Answers will vary. Sample answer: To inherit everlasting life, you must show mercy and compassion to your

"neighbors," even when they're strangers to you.

141–148. Answers will vary.
149. Answers will vary. Sample answer: The seed that falls on the path stands for people who hear the word of God but don't listen to it. The seed on the rock stands for people who believe for a time but then give in to temptation. The seed that falls into good soil stands for people who hear and obey the word of God.
150–162. Answers will vary.
163. Answers will vary. Sample answer: It tells us that, as well as being deeply spiritual, Muhammad was practical and politically able.
164. Answers will vary.
165. Answers will vary. Sample answer: Muslims saw their prophets as directly involved with their welfare, even

interceding with Allah on their behalf.

166–169. Answers will vary.

170. 1. f, 2. c, 3. j, 4. e, 5. i, 6. b, 7. h, 8. d, 9. a, 10. g

171–178. Answers will vary.

179. Answers will vary. Sample answer: The "experts" failed because they looked at the problem from their own viewpoints, not that of the boy. A small child wouldn't be impressed by the scientific explanation of the eardrums or the ritual explanation of the sacred activity. He wouldn't need meditation to calm him; he wasn't the stressed one. The third and sixth experts offered solutions to the neighbors but didn't address the real problem. The Sufi looked at the problem from the boy's point of view and presented a challenge that a child would respond to. The combination of a question to prompt curiosity and the availability of the tools probably led to the rapid destruction of the drum.

180. Answers will vary.

Turn downtime into learning time!

Other books in the
Daily *Warm-Ups* series:

- Algebra
- Algebra II
- Analogies
- Biology
- Character Education
- Chemistry
- Commonly Confused Words
- Critical Thinking
- Earth Science
- Geography
- Geometry
- Journal Writing
- Math Word Problems

- Mythology
- Physics
- Poetry
- Pre-Algebra
- Prefixes, Suffixes, & Roots
- Shakespeare
- Spelling & Grammar
- Test-Prep Words
- U.S. History
- Vocabulary
- World Cultures
- World History
- Writing